About Sounds True

Sounds True is a multimedia publisher whose mission is to inspire and support personal transformation and spiritual awakening. Founded in 1985 and located in Boulder, Colorado, we work with many of the leading spiritual teachers, thinkers, healers, and visionary artists of our time. We strive with every title to preserve the essential "living wisdom" of the author or artist. It is our goal to create products that not only provide information to a reader or listener, but that also embody the quality of a wisdom transmission.

For those seeking genuine transformation, Sounds True is your trusted partner. At SoundsTrue.com you will find a wealth of free resources to support your journey, including exclusive weekly audio interviews, free downloads, interactive learning tools, and other special savings on all our titles.

To learn more, please visit SoundsTrue.com/bonus/free_gifts or call us toll free at 800-333-9185.

AWAKEN
the INNER
SHAMAN

JOSÉ LUIS STEVENS, PhD

AWAKEN the INNER SHAMAN

A Guide to the Power Path
of the Heart

sounds true
BOULDER, COLORADO

Sounds True
Boulder, CO 80306

Published 2014

Cover design by Jennifer Miles
Book design by Beth Skelley

Printed in the United States of America

Library of Congress Cataloging-in-Publication Data
Stevens, Jose Luis.
  Awaken the Inner Shaman : a guide to the power path of the heart / Jose
Luis Stevens.
     pages cm
  Includes bibliographical references.
  ISBN 978-1-62203-093-4
  1. Shamanism. 2. Spiritual healing—Shamanism. 3. Mental healing.
  I. Title.
  BL2370.S5S74 2014
  201'.44--dc23
                                                2013037898

eBook ISBN: 978-1-62203-170-2

10 9 8 7 6 5 4 3 2

To the one and only Inner Shaman,
shared by everyone

Knowing others is wisdom;
Knowing the self is enlightenment.

LAO TZU, *Tao Te Ching,* Sutra 33

CONTENTS

PREFACE

This book has not fallen into your hands or appeared on your screen at this particular time accidentally. Nothing is truly accidental. And yet, this book may not be for everyone. It is for those of you who place the greatest value on personal freedom, who have limitless curiosity for learning about the universe, who yearn to explore the great mystery of life. It is for those of you who are interested in deconstructing your habitual sense of reality to become free from the retaining walls of the mind. If you are content with the status quo of your life, if you don't want to question what you have been taught, if you don't want to rock the boat and want to remain simply comfortable in your life, then please ignore this book. This book is about transformation. It is about changing your life, breaking out of simple comforts and into something far greater. Reading it will upset your apple cart.

But, if you are interested in the greatest journey ever taken, then by all means read this book, rock your boat, deconstruct your reality, allow yourself to be presented with information that can drive you to tremendous expansion, unlimited freedom, infinite power, and joyful awareness.

INTRODUCTION

This is a book about awakening the most powerful, creative source within you, a core self that has been with you, inside you, since your ageless beginning. This creative, energized core self has always been operating within you, but acts subtly in the background, like an engine idling. It has been waiting for your acknowledgment so that it has permission to engage and release its immense power and influence in your life.

This creative source within you is what I call the Inner Shaman. The deep self has been referred to by many names over the ages. You may know it as Essence, Spirit, Soul, Source, Core Self, I Am, the Way, the Tao, the Christ force, or, perhaps more accurately, by no name at all. I prefer to call it the Inner Shaman because shamanism is the world's most ancient understanding of the power within. This power within is that which is most true about you—and yet it draws no attention to itself, which is impressive. You are unaware of it. Think of yourself as sitting on a nuclear reactor and not knowing it is there. It is that powerful; it holds that much potential for radical change. This is a testament to its willingness to grant you absolute freedom to acknowledge it or not, to choose it or not, to harness its awesome power or not. The Inner Shaman never coerces, demands, or fights you. It offers no resistance to your thoughts or feelings; rather, it accepts them fully as you wend your way through life.

That said, not all of your thoughts and feelings are in harmony with it, resonate with it, or support its authenticity. The Inner Shaman tolerates these distractions because it is not threatened by them and is in no way harmed by them. In fact, your Inner Shaman ignores most of your experience, just as you might ignore the distant drone of a small plane that has nothing to do with your current focus. By ignoring your experience, it does not intend to be cruel or abandon you; in fact, you benefit from it ignoring your worries, conflicts, judgments, fears, disappointments, and angers. The Inner Shaman simply waits for your sanity, that glimmer of light or recognition on your part. In short, it is waiting for your readiness to be aware of it. Until that moment of your maturity, when the seed within germinates and casts off its outer husk, the Inner Shaman abides. In the meantime, it does not interfere, nor does it encourage anything that lacks power, heart, and true meaning.

Because your Inner Shaman is connected with the truth, it is not fearful; therefore, it is that part of you that is courageous, that part of you that cannot be discouraged, does not become anxious, does not become depressed. In short, your Inner Shaman is that aspect of you that is completely healthy. It is filled with an infinite supply of vitality, creativity, curiosity, inspiration, and deep inner knowing about the appropriate course of action for your life. The Inner Shaman helps you to let go of your need to control yourself and others, and helps you to relax and trust that you are held safely in the arms of life itself. There *is* a meaningful plan for you; the Inner Shaman knows exactly what that is and will inexorably lead you to it. The only thing that can deter you is fear.

Discovering your Inner Shaman will help you to override any tendency to feel like a victim, to feel disempowered, to fall into laziness and lack of motivation. Embracing the Inner Shaman will make you more efficient and more productive as you systematically erase the energy leaks in your life. Worry is an energy leak, as is being concerned with what others think or how they see you. The Inner Shaman does not care. And yet, at the same time, the Inner Shaman is the energy of love.

I have chosen to refer to this powerful core of being as the Inner Shaman because I believe this is the best, most accurate description. Shamans are unique and powerful individuals who operate in indigenous cultures in every continent. They have existed since the beginning of history. Through an inner calling and their own hard work and initiative, shamans perform critical service for their communities. They are known by many other names: *maracame* among the Huichol of Mexico, man or woman of knowledge in the Toltec tradition in southern Mexico, *paqo* in the Andes of Peru and Bolivia, medicine man or woman in North American tribes, and many more. In modern times, "shaman" has become the generic name for these powerful teachers, philosophers, and healers. They are the world's oldest spiritual leaders, individuals who, among their many duties, heal the sick, perform ceremonies to harmonize the community with the environment, battle negativity, communicate with the ancestors, work with allies for the good of others, gather knowledge, teach through storytelling, act as seers and prophets, and lead their people. They spend a great deal of time gathering power and energy to perform complex supernatural feats and travel to other dimensions and distant locations, such as the star cluster the Pleiades, located in the constellation of Taurus, also known as the Seven Sisters, to gather knowledge and experience. This path, the shamanic path, is first and foremost a path of heart, service, and generosity, and the love of Spirit and all creation. It is also the path of balance. Shamans the world over strive to live in complete harmony with nature, the environment, the cycles of the seasons, the weather, and the varying patterns of the stars, moon, and sun. To accomplish this, they cultivate the intelligence of the heart. Within the heart lies the clarity of mind to see with expert knowledge of this world and worlds beyond.

While some shamans fall prey to greed, power, and the dark arts—which is true in any profession—as a group, shamans are the people who take the greatest responsibility for the well-being of the planet and all its inhabitants, including animals, plants, and all the elements. Equally, shamans hold great care and responsibility for the spiritual realms. Although most of these practitioners do not admit they are shamans, to refer to them as such is offering them the greatest compliment, the highest of honors.

"Shaman" is an ancient word from the Evenki tribe in Siberia, a reindeer people, and it means "the one who sees in the dark," or "the one who knows." The Inner Shaman is the core awareness, the wise one within you who knows and sees the truth, who walks in beauty and balance, who has access to infinite knowledge, infinite power, and infinite tranquility. What better name could there be?

MY JOURNEY OF DISCOVERY

My own journey toward reconnecting with my Inner Shaman was a long and circuitous one. As a child I was introduced to the great shamans of the Bible, who demonstrated their knowledge of the Inner Shaman in acts of heroism and enormous compassion. Moses, at the direction of Spirit, parted the waters of the Red Sea, directed a rain of hail, and drew forth water from a rock. Jesus cast out devils, calmed tempests, changed water into wine, healed the sick, and appeared to his apostles after his crucifixion. These stories of shifting the normal laws of physics, directing and harnessing the forces of nature, introduced me to the enormous powers of the awakened heart.

I attended a Jesuit university during the late sixties, where I was introduced to the great religions and philosophies of the world. After reading the story of his life in *Autobiography of a Yogi*, I began to study the powerful teachings of Yogananda. For the first time I realized that miracles had often been performed by people outside the Christian tradition. At Berkeley, where I went to graduate school in clinical social work, I was fortunate to be introduced to the Korean Zen master Seung Sahnime, a joyful, round-faced teacher who in his broken English managed to convey to me an entirely different perspective. I will never forget him pointing to his shiny bald head in response to my questions and saying lightheartedly, "Too many thinking. Put it all down. Only go straight; keep don't-know mind." Then he laughed with tremendous mirth. These were, I was to find out later, the basics of the shamanic approach to life. Much later, I was to discover that Master Seung was the most exalted Zen master in all Korea and world-renowned. Little did I know!

I began to read voraciously, diving into the world of metaphysics and the perennial philosophy, the understanding that one truth underlies all the world's major religions. I read Annie Besant, C. W. Leadbeater, Madame Blavatsky, Alice Bailey, Manly Hall, and Aldous Huxley. Jane Roberts's channeled Seth books turned my view of reality on its head. It was the first time I encountered the concept that I created my own reality. This is a basic principle in shamanic understanding.

After completing my social work studies at Berkeley, I needed thousands of hours of experience to get licensed, so I got a job at Napa State Mental Hospital in California on a locked ward for adolescents. For two tough years I worked with young people suffering from severe mental illness. Then, emotionally exhausted and just twenty-eight years old, I decided to head to the Far East on a solo quest for adventure. In India and Thailand, I met people who demonstrated supernormal abilities to alter the conventional laws of nature. I saw people walk on fire and glass, bend heavy steel with their concentration, foretell the future, and demonstrate the ability to simply know things about me that no one could have told them. Witnessing these events excited me, relieved me, unnerved me, and produced profound disorientation all at the same time. My world was rocked—and I knew that this new way of seeing was what I longed for most.

In Nepal, I met and studied with a Tibetan Buddhist lama who taught me that learning involves much more than hearing words; he simply downloaded knowledge into me by pressing his forehead into mine. In Varanasi, India, I had a life reading that foretold my future with surprising accuracy and helped to save my life much later in my journey. At the time, being told how and when I was going to die sent me into a spiral of anxiety and depression. Fortunately, I was to learn that I could change these seemingly fixed plans, and now I have outlived the date of my foretold demise by many years. Through my shamanic practice, I recovered my freedom to choose my future.

When I returned home, I suffered from culture shock. To make sense of all that had transpired on my travels, I began to study with a man whom many in my circle were talking about, Reverend Lewis Bostwick. He didn't look the part: he was a portly man in overalls with no formal education who had started the Berkeley Psychic Institute in an old house, where he held informal classes. He taught me a great deal about the Inner Shaman, although the terms he used were "God of your heart" and "space." He made me aware of the enormous power of the inner self and demonstrated time and again what it could do. He could read just about anyone's mind. With a flick of his hand, he could remove a negative thought or a programmed pattern. Although I held a master's degree, I felt I was in kindergarten in this new pursuit of knowledge.

In 1980, I decided it was time to get my doctorate in psychology, and chose the California Institute of Asian Studies (now CIIS) in San Francisco. Here I was exposed to men and women who had studied with shamans, which led me and my wife, Lena, to apprentice for ten years with Guadalupe Candelario, a Huichol shaman or maracame. The Huichol live in the rugged sierras of central Mexico and are one of only two tribes who managed to escape conquest by the Spaniards and keep their way of life. Among their people are many men and women who practice the old traditions and are renowned for their knowledge and expertise in shamanism. For over ten years, we drove over a thousand miles to central Mexico to work with Guadalupe in secrecy. We were to tell no one, not even our friends, that we were engaged in this apprenticeship. Sometimes he would come up to the States to work with us on our home turf. In the beginning, the apprenticeship was hard for me because Guadalupe ignored me and spoke only to Lena. After several years, he saw I was truly committed and embraced me in earnest. I had gone down the rabbit hole so deep I could never go back to the way I had once been.

The Huichol are also known for their powerful healing ceremonies, in which they consume large quantities of the hallucinogenic cactus peyote, chant, and dance without stopping for days on end. During one all-night ceremony, Guadalupe shared a personal story that forever changed me. He spoke of how his father had been murdered when he was a child and how his mother had run off with the murderer, leaving him and his brothers and sisters to fend for themselves. Abandoned and impoverished in a small mountain village, he took on the responsibility to raise his siblings, and he had to rely on Spirit to help him. They survived by begging and doing little jobs. Later, as a teenager, he lived with his aunt, an accomplished maracame, who taught him the shamanic ways of the Huichol. She sent him into the wilderness for three years on a walkabout to meet the Inner Shaman; when he returned, he became a teacher/shaman to his own people. I was truly inspired and impressed that this illiterate man had become the sterling teacher that he was. I realized that if he could meet with such challenges and emerge stronger, certainly I could deal with my much better circumstances and realize my dreams as well.

Many years later, Lena and I met a powerful Huichol maracame as we were walking to a special ceremony for the healing of children. This seemingly simple Indio in a sombrero and tattered clothes, leading a donkey, greeted us on the mountain trail with the words, "And what has God told you today?" Taken a little aback, I smiled and sputtered something. He then regaled us with a lengthy account of what God had told him. His words revealed to us an understanding of the world and future events unknown to many so-called educated people. He spoke of upcoming economic chaos and the need to return to a natural way of life. He spoke of climate change and the need to change our ways before it is too late. He spoke of drought and wars and the need to connect with Spirit because without that there will be no solution. Many of his prophecies have come to pass over the years. I have never forgotten that spontaneous meeting and how his eyes revealed the depth of his knowing. As the shamans would say, this seemingly chance meeting was no accident. We had a date with destiny that day and were meant to cross paths. He did not get his information from books or newscasts. He simply listened to Spirit, to his Inner Shaman, and knew.

In 1990 I moved with my family to Santa Fe, New Mexico, where I still reside. I met Native Americans of many tribes through ceremonies, sweat lodges, and classes. I found this to be both inspiring and painful, as I experienced the backlash of hostility engendered by the terrible history of the Indians' treatment at the hands of white people. This is partly what drove me to study with shamans of other cultures, who were much more willing to share their teachings with me.

My knowledge of the Inner Shaman was broadened through countless trips to Peru to work with the Shipibo of the Upper Amazon, who have a reputation as the go-to people for those who want to learn shamanism in the jungle. The Shipibo are world-class singers and ceremonialists, downloading song patterns from nature and weaving them into exquisite textiles and painting them on their clothing and buildings. The Shipibo introduced me to the power of the Inner Shaman through song, prayer, ceremony, and many days and nights of special plant diets that opened up inner worlds of vision and power. Before I met the Shipibo, I hardly ever sang. Now I sing every day as part of my practice and it makes me happy, as it is meant to.

Likewise, for many years I have studied with the Q'ero paqos, the shamans of the rugged Andean mountains of Peru. Like the Huichol, they were able to escape the Spanish conquest by fleeing to the high mountains, where they continued to practice the oldest traditions of the Incas and preserve their powerful knowledge. Visiting the Q'ero is no easy task and requires navigating mountain passes over 17,000 feet. Even in the warmer months, the altitude makes it bitterly cold. Having few or no plants, the Q'ero are masters of healing with the mineral kingdom, masters of the weather, and are able to communicate with the *apus*, the great guardian peaks of the Andes. On any number of occasions I have seen them communicate with the clouds and arrange for a fierce storm to go around us so that we could finish a *despacho*, a gift offering to the mountains, or continue our journey on a mountain trail.

After one of my extraordinary trips to Peru, while looking out of the plane window as we circled to land in Albuquerque,

New Mexico, I felt the most intense communication with the desert landscape spread out below me. The land was welcoming me home in a way I had never experienced before. The Inner Shaman revealed to me that I was not the same person who had left three weeks before, that because of the difficult tobacco diet I had undertaken I was opened to ways of seeing and knowing that had previously been sealed off from me. This has never left me. Thus, as time has passed, the Inner Shaman has gone from being an interesting idea to becoming my personal reality.

I have learned more about the Inner Shaman by visiting the aboriginal shamans in Australia, the Sami people in Finland, and the Maya in Guatemala. The Maya especially helped me to appreciate shamans' ability to read the stars, do intricate math, and create calendar systems that are uncannily accurate over billions of years. Perhaps no one has predicted the future so profoundly and accurately as they have. Few people know that according to the Maya elders, the sixty years after 2012 hold the key to this planet's future; the world will go through such a dramatic transformation that it will be hardly recognizable by 2072. This will be for the great good of mankind. Much of the time in between will be something like a construction zone, with chaos as old systems collapse and are replaced by better ones.

The world is changing rapidly, and there is no going back to the value paradigm of the recent past: "He who dies with the most toys wins." The world's economies and energy practices will change to more sustainable models, international relations will shift toward more cooperation, social systems—from education to medicine to governance—will change for the better. You will find in this book what you need on the inside to navigate the coming times, but you will have to do your part and put the information to work if you wish to evolve. It can be great fun and infinitely rewarding.

Knowledge of the Inner Shaman has been around for centuries, but only a few revolutionary individuals were capable of grasping it and implementing it in the modern world. Now a powerful portal has opened, a window of opportunity that makes this knowledge critical. Take advantage of it; time is short. You are at a choice point. Which reality do you want to follow? Which future do you want to experience? I can tell you that the path of the Inner Shaman is a future that will manifest in cooperation, gratitude, forgiveness, and love.

The short history I have related here by no means references all the wonderful teachers I have met in my life who have broadened my understanding of who and what the Inner Shaman is. They have all been part of my journey, a stupendous experience, at times filled with the most difficult frustration, fear, doubt, and impatience on the one hand and unbounded joy, passion, awe, and exuberance on the other. No doubt, should you decide to take a similar journey of discovering the Inner Shaman, you will undergo your own powerful transformation. That possibility inspires me and helps me to fulfill my life task as a pivotal facilitator for personal growth and acceleration. It is my motivation for writing this book. I hope that your life path will be even more powerful than mine has been and certainly as rewarding. My intention is that you find joy, fulfillment, satisfaction, and grand mystery on this fabulous journey.

ADDRESSING DOUBT

It is natural to have doubts about the existence of the Inner Shaman, so I will address these up front. Perhaps you have never seen or felt the Inner Shaman in the course of your everyday affairs. Why should you even give it the time of day when there is no direct evidence for it in your life? Healthy skepticism is a good thing, as it gets your curiosity up and leads you to investigate and expand in order to learn. You want to make sure something is true or accurate before you put your faith in it. This is the thinking behind sound research, clinical trials for medications, and many other procedures that have prevented countless deaths and injuries. Unhealthy skepticism is a dismissal of anything new, anything different from your everyday programming and belief system. Galileo was met with unhealthy skepticism when he discovered that the earth orbited the sun; the Catholic Church was fearful that this new thinking would contradict the word of God and lead followers astray. When motorized transport was invented, some people were afraid they would die from lack of oxygen if they went over twenty-five miles per hour. For years, no one thought homeopathic medicine could be effective simply because they did not understand how it worked. Examples of unhealthy skepticism are legion, but in the end it never prevails. The truth wins out.

I experienced unhealthy skepticism when I met a highly successful oil baron who, when I mentioned the Inner Shaman to him, told me, "Well, if it really existed I would have heard about it already." He was suggesting that he already knew everything worth knowing and therefore he had nothing left to learn.

The Inner Shaman is a grave threat to the status quo, the world run by false personality—ego, as the Buddhists frame it, or, as the Toltec shamans call it, the parasite. Throughout this book I will refer to this surface personality run by delusion as the false personality or the parasite. Our everyday persona is most often not real or true, and it is parasitical. The false personality is based on the irrational fear that we are ultimately alone in a world that has no meaning or purpose. It tries to take control of our lives by motivating us to micromanage everything and pursue behavior that ultimately leads to the seven deadly obstacles or fears: greed, self-destructiveness, self-deprecation (self-judgment), arrogance, martyrdom, impatience, and stubbornness. According to the Inner Shaman, we were designed to feel good, to experience joy through living. The false personality or parasite tries to take over by creating suffering, never-ending craving, disease, injury, defensiveness, selfishness, and fear-based behavior. When you feel bad in these ways, you can know that you are somehow under the influence of the false personality. When you feel fulfilled, inspired, awakened, and genuinely good, you can be sure you are under the influence of the Inner Shaman. Because this is such a simple dichotomy, you would think that people would avidly avoid feeling bad and constantly move toward feeling good, but as you can readily see, this is not the case. The false personality has deluded people into thinking that feeling bad is actually good, and feeling good is actually bad. What a ruse!

The Inner Shaman, on the other hand, is more powerful than any false surface self, any parasite, and certainly any human organization. It is more powerful than religion, government, the UN, the CIA, the FBI, the KGB, political parties, the military–industrial complex, the educational system, the health care system, or any terror organization on the planet. Because of this power it is perceived to be an enormous threat, and thus for eons there have been massive efforts to stamp out any reference to it, any acknowledgment of it, any admission of its existence. Vast organizations have tried to provide substitutes, to distract people and control them. They say that you need an intermediary to communicate with the source or the creator of your experience—a priest, minister, imam, or rabbi—because you don't have the status, the power, the resources, the education, or more importantly the right to connect with Spirit yourself. As well as the world's largest religions, the military–industrial complex, the scientific community, the corporate world, and powerful political parties such as the Nazis, the Fascists, and the Communists have tried to stamp out all references to the Inner Shaman. Hitler had shamans rounded up and sent to the camps.

The everyday world offers its own substitutes and distractions in the forms of entertainment, shopping, sex, food, and money. None of these can hold a candle to the awakened Inner Shaman, yet they have proven to be effective in keeping the populace asleep until recently. Now the Inner Shaman is beginning to stir en masse, activating specifically through human DNA. With that emergence comes an awesome awareness. The reason it is emerging at this time is very simple: subconsciously or consciously, we want it to; we have asked it to. As a populace, we are becoming tired of a world that does not work, a world that promises everything but delivers precious little of actual joyfulness, bliss, and satisfaction. Last time I noticed, flat-screen TVs, cell phones, computers, and the latest-model cars have raised the standard of living but have not produced happiness. The more difficult the circumstances of the world become, the more ready we are for the manifestation of the Inner Shaman within us. In our deepest core we yearn for the ultimate truth, though we may not be able to name it. We yearn to connect with Spirit here and now, to unleash the hidden powers that are our birthright and that have been manifested by only a few of the greatest historical avatars and spiritual masters. In our hearts we want to be healers and miracle workers—"walking blessings," as the Q'ero call the greatest shamans among them. We want to have the power and influence to serve and solve the problems of inequality, poverty, war, and hunger. We want to talk to nature and listen as it talks back to us and teaches us the ways of happiness. As you will see, this yearning is built right into our DNA—and it will never go away.

HOW TO APPROACH THIS BOOK

This book is organized in a logical manner; each chapter builds upon what came before. Therefore, it will make the most sense if you read it through from beginning to end first. After that, you can return to any chapter that appeals to you, or to exercises that you might like to do repeatedly. You may find it valuable to just let the book fall open wherever it may. (A tip: I like to reward readers of my books by putting some of the best information near the end, because someone who has persevered deserves the deepest gems.) However, you will find important and valuable information in all parts of this book. Enjoy.

1

QUANTUM PHYSICS
and the INNER SHAMAN

Because you are probably like me, you may need a little science to help you understand shamanism. So here we will discuss, in a limited sort of way, what quantum physics has to say about the reality of the Inner Shaman. If you feel you are well acquainted with this topic, you can skip ahead to the next chapter.

As most of quantum physics is either still entirely theoretical or waiting for hard evidence, not all competent physicists agree or even believe in quantum physics. Many spiritually oriented people claim that quantum physics offers proof of their spiritual beliefs, but this is just not so—because the measuring stick of science is too small to prove anything about spirituality. Nevertheless, I will try to explain the Inner Shaman in terms of the theories that quantum physicists currently believe to be correct. Bear in mind that all this could change in a heartbeat.

1

By now most quantum physicists are in agreement that the entire atomic structure of the known universe exists within a context that they call the quantum field. The quantum field is that out of which everything springs into manifestation and into which everything returns and disappears. According to astrophysicists, a big bang occurred that sent matter rocketing in every direction to form planets, moons, suns, and galaxies; the big bang is said to have sprung from the quantum field, a kind of zero point with no temperature, no time, and no space. Within a millisecond after the big bang, 96 percent of all the matter created was sucked back into the quantum field and seemed to vanish. The other 4 percent went on to make up the structures of our universe. Astrophysicists speculate that the 96 percent that vanished still exists in the form of invisible antimatter—which remains a theoretical construct.

If the entire universe sprang from one point, then the quantum field is misnamed. It is not really a field but, as the Hindus call it, a *bindu* point, which represents what they have called the great void and what the ancient Chinese called the Tao. The void is, paradoxically, nowhere and everywhere, and exists outside of everything known, outside of space and time. It is thus very difficult to discuss. The Chinese say that the Tao that can be named is not the Tao. Given this, the big bang theory, when all is said and done, is probably bogus. According to shamans, the physical universe was dreamed up and may be perpetually changing in form. The truth is, no one knows for sure. Use your intuition here. Does a big bang make sense to you? Does it correspond to anything else that you know to be true? Does anything come from nothing? On the other hand, in dreams anything is possible, including a big bang.

THE PORTABLE CENTER OF THE UNIVERSE

Quantum physicists say that particles that emerge from the quantum field are affected by observation. Without an observer, a particle is a wave and may appear anywhere in the universe. The instant the particle is observed, it assumes a fixed position in time and space and is no longer a wave. In other words, the particles that make up every structure in the universe depend on an observer to become something we can perceive. It is not a stretch, therefore, to say that we are dreamers dreaming our world by specifying locations for particles with our consciousness. This is, of course, what shamans and mystics have been saying for thousands of years. The master of ceremonies, the ultimate dreamer, is the Inner Shaman, who wants nothing more than to create harmony, balance, and an experience of utter bliss. The world we experience is not always harmonic, balanced, and blissful because of the distortions created by the false personality, a subject we will cover at length. Erase the fiction of the false personality and what we have left is pure truth, love, and energy.

Quantum physicists have determined that the shape of the universe is a torus, like a huge donut or smoke ring. Imagine that the smoke ring is circulating smoke down through the center, around the bottom, up the sides, and then around the top into the hole and down again. Let us say that the universe is being created when the energy, or smoke, is ejected from the hole at the bottom. Therefore, if you were underneath the smoke ring, it would appear as if all of creation were being ejected from the hole in the sky above you. The ancient Hindus said that all of creation comes from the bindu point, and in sacred geometry creation is seen as the central sun, a dot with a circle around it. Sounds like a torus, doesn't it?

As the energy progresses up the sides of the torus and goes over the top, it sucks everything down the center again, like a giant black hole. Here is where the universe disappears. So the giant torus is at the same time a hole of creation and a hole of destruction, a principle symbolized by Shiva and Shakti, the Hindu gods of creation and destruction.

Now imagine, as quantum physicists speculate, that every photon of light radiating from atoms has a tiny torus at the center of it, where the light appears and disappears infinitely. At the exact center on the inside of the hole is a spot where one set of energy or light disappears and one appears. What exactly is behind it? Physicists don't know. They suggest possible multiple universes or parallel realities, and this may be so. Somewhere, somehow, they will have to account for what is behind all those other universes and realities. Shamans are clear about what is back there. They say it is Spirit, the Source, the Almighty, or simply God. Cross-culturally, shamans also say that the center of the universe is portable and is anywhere we say it is, even multiple places at once. So consequently, according to their view, Spirit is everywhere.

Energetically speaking, shamans conceive of the heart as being in the exact center of what some call a luminous egg but could also be called a torus. In your heart, then, is the bindu point, the creation point, the place where it all happens. Of course, this is where the Inner Shaman is going to be. However, we would do well to remember that at the center of every particle of the universe is a torus, or, in other words, a center of the universe replicated millions and millions of times over. How can there be more than one center of the universe? For shamans this is easy. The universe is a hologram in which every point equals every other point. The whole universe can be produced at any point within it. What gives shamans their power is their ability to be in the exact center of the universe at will. This is what they mean when they say that, when all is said and done, there is only one child of the Great Spirit. It only appears that there are many.

2

HOW the INNER SHAMAN WORKS with DNA

Information in almost every field imaginable is exploding—growing and expanding at an unprecedented speed. It has been calculated that our knowledge base is growing so fast that the amount of information that once took 1,000 years to be discovered subsequently was discovered in the next 500 years, then 250 years, then 125 years, until now 1,000 years of information is learned in only a few days. Soon this mathematical progression will diminish to some infinitesimal amount of time, and the amount of information will be infinite.

The linear mind, or left hemisphere of the brain, cannot grasp the implications of this, so we must rely on the right hemisphere, which is capable of multidimensional thought. If we realize that there is no real vacuum in space, that it is filled with infinite information, we can see that we are already surrounded and interpenetrated by information. Through the process of induction, infinitely overlapping magnetic fields instantly inform our own small biological magnetic field and we become privy to all information everywhere in the universe. This has always been so; we just didn't realize it. This is the knowledge that all the great and enlightened masters discovered: that they had access to all the knowledge in the universe at the tips of their fingers—or, more accurately, in the middle of their chests, where the Inner Shaman resides. Jesus, Buddha, Krishna, and Lao Tzu (to name just a few) knew this.

Let us examine this more deeply, so that you can clearly understand the good fortune of what you have available to you: the tremendous power spoken of in sacred books and by great teachers throughout the ages. When you work on a puzzle, it is often easiest to begin with the frame and then fill in the middle pieces until you have a complete picture. So let us begin at the edges and travel toward the center, bringing the picture together.

Only in the last fifteen years have we been able to map the human genome, and to some extent decode it. Humans have about 23,000 pairs of genes, similar to our cousin the chimpanzee—fewer genes than some plants. In fact, if you look at the early embryos of a turtle, a snake, a monkey, a chicken, and a human being, it is hard to tell them apart. So what is it that happens over time that causes them to turn out so differently?

Only 10 percent of the human genome seems to be in sequence. The other 90 percent was classified as junk DNA, because the researchers could see no use for it. Only recently have they begun to discover that these junk genes are like switches that turn other genes on and off as needed. Human beings have a gene for a tail, but it is switched off; other animals have genes that are switched on in humans but switched off for them. This is why embryos that look so similar grow into entirely different creatures with entirely different capacities.

Scientists are now realizing that there is no junk in the gene pool, only that which was not understood at first.

Why are we talking about genes? Because genes are biological carriers of information, and give us access to an infinite amount of information within our own bodies. The entire history of the human race is to be found in our gene pool, but that is not all. Each gene has a tiny magnetic field, and all together they have a larger magnetic field. Since all magnetic fields in the universe overlap and instantly, totally share information, you have access to all information in the universe via your genes. Your genes carry information about every past life, every lesson learned, every agreement kept, where you think you are now and who you think you are at this moment. Thus your genome is a multidimensional library of personal, global, and spiritual identity. Your genes, embedded in every cell of your body, are your library card to the universe. Your genes are not just *about* you; they are closer to the real you than you can imagine. Your genome is unique to you; at the same time, it is hooked into the same information that the genomes of all other people are hooked into. So, are you really separate from other people? No! The difference among people, beyond their selected physical traits, is that some are more aware of the information they have access to than others. That is all.

What part does the Inner Shaman play in this? In some ways, the Inner Shaman is indistinguishable from your gene pool. You could also say that the Inner Shaman is the organizing principle behind it. Having this powerhouse inside your skin does not necessarily mean that you use all its features. You could; they are available. But you haven't yet. There is no question that at some point you will, because that is where evolution is rapidly taking us all.

Imagine a computer loaded with powerful software. In order to access these programs, you would have to give the computer the proper commands; then whole new dimensions would open up to you. If you don't know the programs are there, they remain dormant and you may never be aware of anything beyond the simple programs you use every day.

Right now, 95 percent of human beings do not consciously use their genes to capacity. This is a shame, because everyone has within themselves the tools to solve most of their problems, especially health problems. Most people use less than one-third of their gene potential. For the most part, humans have not been mature enough to use all these features until now. Now is the great turning point; we are currently shifting from young soul to mature soul awareness. Puberty is all about learning to use a much greater set of tools, isn't it?

Let us now turn toward another part of the puzzle. Several of the world's most sacred books make reference to "the Word." In the Bible, the Gospel according to John starts, "In the beginning was the Word." The Word is sound: a specific vibration that with intention causes something to rise up out of the quantum field and become manifest. All the great shamanic traditions refer to this concept: the power of utterance, of sound, of vibration, of creation. Sound, or vibration, exists everywhere we look in this universe. The Inner Shaman is sound, vibration, word, and this is how it interfaces with the great chorus of humming DNA that not only makes up your cells but the field all around you.

The Word refers to action, the male aspect of God. The void is the feminine face of God. It has everything but specifies nothing. It is utter peace or chaos. To be specific, to differentiate one aspect of the void from another, requires the masculine face of God: thought, intention, creation, action. It has been said that human beings are made in the likeness of their creator. Human beings are capable of creating intention through concentration and focus, are able to voice their intentions, and have access to the knowledge base of the universe through their gene pool.

The genes need communication in order to come to life. On the biological layer, they act from instinct and play out without our conscious awareness; the program is already embedded and activated by the time we are born. We grow into men or women with particular physical characteristics. This instinctive level of gene activation is the one that most people are using. It is very basic—like the primitive software that is bundled into an inexpensive computer.

Downloading more software requires both the knowledge that you can do so and the desire to do so. To be motivated, you usually have to be curious and also have a need. If your life has no meaning, you will have no curiosity and no need. If you feel worthless or martyred, you won't follow up. If you are afraid of change, you will not follow through. If you are arrogant and judgmental, you will be led astray. If you are greedy or impatient, you will not be efficient and won't get the job done. But if you have a desire to evolve and grow and discover the secrets of the universe, if you feel worthy, and if you have a burning need, you will be motivated to do so. In the past, these were the people who became the great masters. This could be you, as well—or, we should say, this will be you! Perhaps this is you now. It is only a matter of time. The window of opportunity is now open.

Let us now put this all together to build the whole picture. You come fully equipped from birth to go way beyond your instincts. You have the power of the word, the action component of Spirit or God. The word is the command you need to activate the programs in your gene pool. You have access to the Inner Shaman, who coordinates your genes. You have free will, so you can decide to proceed any time you want. You have the capacity for vast and rapid change, unlike the plants and animals who are more hooked into instinct. They are here to serve and evolve rather slowly. You are here to evolve rapidly, as in sudden transformation. You are here to work with both ends of the spectrum: the sheer infinity of the quantum field and your fleshy biological base. You are here to exercise choice and go where no woman or man has gone before.

Remember, your genes respond to your intentions and your commands: your word. You need to talk to your genes. Your body is an elemental, a force of nature, and designed to take instructions. Through your genes, your body has access to information that can inform it and remind it of more effective ways of functioning. The Inner Shaman resides in your heart space and is that part of you that is in complete communication with your gene pool at all times. However, your Inner Shaman will not act on your gene pool without your permission. That is why having a relationship with the beloved Inner Shaman is so important: you speak to your genes and the cells of your body via the catalyst that is your Inner Shaman. Everyone has one, no exceptions. It is what makes you unique among the creatures on this planet—not better, just unique. It gives you access to Spirit or, as the shamans call it, the spirit world, where all power resides. It is your pipeline to the universe.

EXERCISE ACTIVATING THE DNA THROUGH THE INNER SHAMAN

1. Find a private, quiet space and get comfortable. You may sit or stand.

2. You may address your Inner Shaman or you may address your genes directly, whichever feels right. In the end, it is the same. You can read this statement or read it over and paraphrase it yourself: "Inner Shaman: I know you are connected to all aspects of my gene pool that is actively interfacing with the quantum field at this very moment. I am so grateful and thankful for all you have done for me throughout my life, for providing for me even when

I was ignorant of your presence and for keeping me going even when I was foolish.

Activating my capacity through my word, I am now giving you permission to fully activate all levels of my genes' capacities for my optimum health, for fully completing my life task work, and for the highest level of happiness and satisfaction that I can manifest in this life."

3. You may end here, or you may go on further with specific intentions. Here are some options: "I give you full permission to activate those aspects of my genes that will rapidly heal this injury, condition, symptom, or disease. May I learn the lesson that precipitated it, quickly through my dreams or directly through my perception and direct knowing of the truth."

Place your right hand vertically in front of your chest, palm facing left, and say, "I am in my knowing now."

And/or:
"At this time I call forth the mastery of X I have attained in any past life that I can put to use now for Y project or Z situation. Thank you for transferring this immediately and fully."

Place your right hand vertically in front of your chest, palm facing left, and say, "I am in my knowing now."

And/or:
"Activate and access all knowledge that will help me know at this time what is the best course of action for me about X."

Place your right hand vertically in front of your chest, palm facing left, and say, "I am in my knowing now."

And/or:
"Activate the perfect template, the original blueprint for my optimum health, the healing of my body completely at this time. I thank all my helpers and projected aspects of my essence for all the powerful support and help in healing, nourishing and replenishing my cells, renewing my body, and restoring every detail to optimal fitness, flexibility, and energy level. Raise my amplitude, my vibration, and my consciousness to the highest level that is right for me at this time. Support me to discover quickly my optimum service to the world."

Place your right hand vertically in front of your chest, palm facing left, and say, "I am in my knowing now."

3

THE INNER SHAMAN and ITS POWERFUL TASK

As you have just seen, through the multidimensional and quantum aspects of your DNA, the Inner Shaman is wholly connected with all that is—the Tao, the logos, or, in other words, the source of the universe. Since the Inner Shaman is part of the Tao, it *is* the Tao, because according to the ancient Chinese Taoists, the Tao cannot be divided. Being a *part* of everything is actually impossible, because each part is also everything. Thus, your Inner Shaman *is* everything, infinite and immortal. Trying to conceive of it as separate from you is like trying to separate out a part of the ocean with a fish net and calling it something else. It's either ocean or it's not. The job of the Inner Shaman is to resonate with the Tao, match wills with the Tao, intend what the Tao intends, match the Tao in amplitude, light, and creativity, dream with the Tao, and finally, extend the Tao.

The results of the work of your Inner Shaman are extraordinary: the blossoming forth of your awareness, your consciousness, and your being. This may sound absolutely outrageous—but in the realm of mysticism, the more outrageous the teaching, the truer it is. The truth is very often stranger than fiction.

There is a famous Buddhist story that illustrates nicely the nature of the Inner Shaman. A young student of Zen heard of a great master who lived as a hermit in a small hut at the peak of a high mountain. Through considerable effort and trial he managed to scale the mountain and arrived at the tiny hermitage. The master greeted him amiably and invited the young student in for tea. Together they entered the stone building and sat at a small table, where a teapot and two teacups were laid out before them. The young man, wishing to impress the Zen master with his knowledge, spoke on and on of his insights and observations. The old master, saying nothing, began pouring the tea. He filled the young monk's cup to the brim and kept pouring, allowing it to overflow. As the young monk continued to talk, the tea flowed onto the table and onto the floor, while the master continued to pour. Finally, losing his patience, the young monk shouted, "You old fool! Can you not see the teacup is full!" The old master replied, "Yes, it is full, just like your mind. If you are to learn anything more, you must empty it out of the old before putting anything more into it."

The Inner Shaman is like that space in the teacup. It is not made up of content, like tea that may come or go; its value is its ability to hold fresh new knowledge.

You can also liken the Inner Shaman to the space that makes up your house. Your space may be filled with furniture, books, clothing, appliances, and untold objects, yet whether the space is filled or not is immaterial to the space. People may move in or move out with their belongings, but the space exists regardless of whose objects are there or whether you fill the space or not. Space is inviolable—and so is the Inner Shaman. The Inner Shaman is more like space or context than anything else. Your local experiences, thoughts, identifications, concerns, feelings, and sensations are like the furniture and objects being moved in and out of the house. They come and go. The space or context does not. It is stable and yet it has no limit, for it is connected to all space. This is what the Zen master wanted to convey to the young monk. Be silent like the space in the cup, not noisy like all the thoughts or the tea spilling on the floor.

The Task of the Inner Shaman and the Triune Universe

The task of the Inner Shaman is to dream the dream of truth on a vast scale. Included in this task is the Inner Shaman's focus on perfectly dreaming up your essence out of all that is. The shamans of the Shuar tribe in the Ecuadorian Amazon jungle teach that life is as we dream it, that yes, we are dreaming it all. All shamans would agree. In this way the Inner Shaman certifies that you are connected to all that is, to the Great Spirit, the Tao, to your Buddha nature, to the Christ force, all of which are your port in a storm. In a word, the Inner Shaman is "home." How is it, then, that human beings become disconnected from such a power source? How can it be that every person has an Inner Shaman but doesn't know it?

Soon we will examine this strange phenomenon in more depth. For now, let us just say that the physical body and its accompanying personality are heavily imprinted by the fixed beliefs of culture, society, and family. These beliefs are like retaining walls in the mind, designed to keep out information and truth. The information that does get in is filtered by your imprinting and conditioning, which distorts the purity of the Inner Shaman's vision of who you are. This distortion is called *maya*, the Hindu word for illusion, which is our human experience of the world. Essentially, you hallucinate your whole life experience, including what you believe to be your identity, all the information you receive through your five senses, the entire physical universe as you perceive it—everything you record as reality. In other words, as the Shuar teach, you are dreaming.

The Inner Shaman's task, in addition to awakening you to the truth of who you are, is to manage a tiny node in the upper right quadrant of the heart called the sino-atrial node. This node holds the electrical impulse that starts and keeps the heart beating when you are an embryo and an infant. As you grow into adulthood, electrical impulses emanate from many places in the heart. Yet within the sino-atrial node there remains a tiny portal to what shamans call the Spirit World—which, invisible to the naked eye, is also known as the quantum field described by physicists.

For shamans the world over, Spirit is the single source of the whole universe: that which is indescribable, perfect, and everywhere. Naturally, there are local names for this ultimate source. Spirits, on the other hand, are the beings that inhabit the universe. Everything has a spirit, so spirits are everywhere: in plants, animals, clouds, mountains, canyons, and so on, including humans. We are all spirits occupying physical forms created by Spirit to express Spirit. Of course, many spirits do not presently occupy physical forms.

The Spirit World is the field that Spirit occupies. It is the source of all power, the source of all energy that keeps the physical world animated and moving. Shamans everywhere say that the physical world is a mere shadow, a mirror image, or an echo of the source of all, located in the Spirit World. The Spirit World contains the blueprints or archetypal plans for everything that ever was, is, or will be. In the Spirit World, everything is available but is as yet unmanifested. It takes a focused consciousness, such as that of a human being, to intend something in order for it to become a physical manifestation.

What propels things into being is intention, attention, and strong emotion. If we are not careful, we can manifest things we are afraid of, because the Spirit World reads resistance the same way it reads desire. According to shamanic wisdom, what you resist is what you become. And be careful what you pray for, because you will manifest it sooner or later! The capacity to dream something into being is an awesome responsibility that deserves respect. Our consciousness makes human beings co-creators with Spirit; the center of this creative activity is in the human heart. This is why many pictures of Jesus and Mary show them pointing to their hearts, and why the order of Sufis, the mystic tradition within Islam, has as its symbol a heart with wings.

The sino-atrial node—the tiny portal in the heart closest to the middle of your chest—contains three filaments, invisible to the naked eye, infinitely finer than the strands of a spider's web. Like fiberoptics, these filaments carry an enormous load of information and power. Their job is to transport three key components from Spirit directly into your heart for distribution through your DNA. The first is truth, or the intelligence of the universe. Your body has the intelligence of the cosmos within it, because truth is piped directly into it via your heart. The second is love, also known as magnetism, which is the force that attracts and holds your form together so that your body has integrity; this is the same force that holds planetary systems and galaxies together. And the third is power, the pure energy that animates you and allows you to carry out all your decisions, actions, and movements. This is what we have already referred to as the action component of God—in the Christian and Hebrew traditions, the Word: the power to choose, to make things happen, to take the consequences of those choices, to have experiences. Without power, without the Word, nothing would happen. According to shamans, this power is neutral, neither good or bad. What we do with it determines its positive or negative influence, according to our experience. The Q'ero of the Andes call the positive aspects *sami* and the inharmonious aspects *hoocha*. Note that hoocha is not considered negative; the Q'ero say only that it is lacking in resonance with what will make us happy.

Together, these three components are known in many different traditions; they are always considered the key building blocks of the visible universe. The triad of the Christian tradition is the Father (love), the Son (truth), and the Holy Spirit (energy). The Inca have the Condor (love), the Serpent (truth), and the Puma (energy). The Huichol name them Corn (love), Deer (truth), and Peyote (energy). In science these three can be found as the majority ingredients of the material universe: oxygen, hydrogen, and nitrogen. Other traditions have symbols that illustrate the triune source of the universe, such as the French fleur-de-lis and the Hindu trident.

In sacred geometry, the triune force is formed, first, by a dot, which represents the Source, the Almighty, the Great Spirit, Allah. This single dot creates an offspring, or replicates itself, thus creating two: Spirit and Spirit's child. This is the beginning of duality, the dynamic tension that creates all we know: through masculine and feminine, cold and hot, strong and weak, and so on. Geometrically speaking, the second dot orbits around its source, describing a circle. The motif of the circle with a dot in the center represented the most sacred teaching in Egyptian, Inca, and other sun-worshipping civilizations. The dot represents the inner, invisible sun, the source; the outer circle represents the external or visible sun, the child. Shamans say it is necessary to bridge the invisible and visible worlds by developing the capacity to be in both places at once, to be in balance.

Three, the number of change, is not a balanced number. It is unstable by nature. Think of how a three-legged stool tends to wobble more than a four-legged chair. This instability creates the illusory motion that we experience as time and movement through space. It is necessary in order for us to have our human experience. The three are aspects of the one; but with one there is nowhere to go and nothing to do. Everything is perfect. When the one takes a tripartite form—pretends to be three—voilà, we have ignition, a physical world with lots of parts to play with. Truth, love, and energy are three. The Inner Shaman is one, the core, the source, and therefore home.

In the science of numerology, the understanding that numbers have symbolic meaning, the number three represents catalytic processes, action, getting things to happen. This physical triune universe is in a constant flow of action, phenomena, events, changes, and transformations. Our world evolves through the mixture and alchemy of truth, love, and energy. Without any one of these, there would no possibility of a physical universe.

THE STABILITY OF THE QUADRANT

Three key components of the universe need a fourth to stabilize them and bring them into dynamic play. In the physical world, which is composed mostly of oxygen, nitrogen, and hydrogen, this fourth component is carbon, which is the primary element composing our bodies. As truth, love, and energy enter the physical world through our hearts (carbon), forms are manifested, animated, and take on temporary stability.

The Inner Shaman is tasked with keeping the flow coming into your heart: the flow of intelligence, the flow of love, and the flow of energy. That flow never stops until the moment of death of your body; if it did, for even a fraction of a second, your body would die immediately. That is how important the Inner Shaman is to your life. It sits within your heart, and in a state of deep concentration and meditation it calls forth this action from Source, from the Spirit World, from all that is. You might be totally unaware of this activity, but with a little attention you may sense that something critical to your life is happening in that location.

The Inner Shaman is the coordinator of the three streams of truth, love, and energy; it is the master of ceremonies, so to speak, of your being. It is the DNA-meister, the director that flips the various DNA switches on and off and determines exactly how you show up as a human being, with your various talents, skills, and limitations. Science cannot yet explain why certain genes are chosen and others are allowed to be latent. The intelligence behind this is your Inner Shaman. The Inner Shaman knows where you came from before this life and where you are headed after it. It knows exactly where you are on your evolutionary path and what is required for you to accelerate to mastery. The Inner Shaman knows because it is designed to know. It is you on a deeper level, far below the local, distracted surface you that gets into all kinds of difficulty and complains about it. It is far more powerful than Superman, Spiderman, or any supernatural action hero.

EXERCISE **PERCEIVING THE THREE STREAMS OF LIFE ENERGY**

One way to perceive these streams of life energy—truth, love, and energy—is to see, sense, or feel them as colors flowing into your heart and then radiating to all the cells of your body. Take a moment to visualize this.

1. Visualize truth as the color of the purest gold, shining, glimmering, shimmering through infinite space and penetrating into the atoms, protons, electrons, and space that make up both the physical aspects of your DNA and its quantum aspects. Ultimately this combination creates the form of your body.

2. Visualize love as rose color, the most beautiful pink of the dawn, also streaming through the cells and atoms of the body and radiating outward through the DNA into an extraordinary egg-shaped halo all around your body, called the luminous egg by Toltec shamans.

3. Visualize power or energy as electric blue in color, the exquisite blue of a candle flame, radiating, pulsing outward, energizing your DNA, your body, and animating your luminous egg. All this the Inner Shaman chooses, actualizes, witnesses, accepts, and allows.

It is important to offer gratitude to the Inner Shaman for these three streams of vital source material, which it provides to you for free, twenty-four/seven. Remember, if any one of them were to cease their flow for even a second, you would cease to exist. The more gratitude you give to Spirit or Source for each stream, the more Spirit will give you. This is how you make them grow. All the great saints discovered that by spending a great deal of time in gratitude for this bounty, they became infinitely richer by the day.

THE INTERDEPENDENCE OF THE THREE STREAMS

Shamans describe the energy field around the human body as the luminous egg because it is egg-shaped and filled with light and color. Carlos Castaneda, who studied with a Yaqui master whom he called Don Juan, described it as a ceramic pot turned on its side with the base in front. The Q'ero call it the *poqpo*, and the Theosophists called it the aura. The three streams of light I described above fill the egg-shaped field with incredible vitality.

These three streams are not as distinct as I have described them, but for the sake of clarity and understanding it is helpful to consider them as separate threads. In truth, they are integral with one another and when they are blended together they emanate the most beautiful violet, the color of the deepest purification, the essence of spirituality.

One way that humans perceive these three streams is through our three primary centers, or chakras: brow center, heart center, and navel center, or head, heart, and gut. From the heart, where the three streams enter, the energy stream flows downward to the gut and the truth stream flows upward to the brow; from there they radiate out to all parts of the body and the energetic field, where they are interpreted into personal expression. In totality, the three centers represent thinking, feeling, and acting, three aspects of being fully human. However, thinking without feeling is cold and calculating, machinelike, and thinking without acting is powerless. Acting without feeling is ruthless, and acting without thinking is insane. Feeling without thinking is directionless, and feeling without acting cannot fully extend itself. Thus, each depends on the others to fulfill its destiny. This is why Spirit provides them, equally and with constancy. It is our responsibility to give these streams the freedom of interaction they are meant to have—and our Inner Shaman guides us in finding and maintaining the inner balance of the three. The heart, being the bridge between the gut and the brow, has a pivotal position when it comes to communication among the three streams. Life can be lived without much heart, but what kind of life is it?

Because we have allowed the false personality a vote in our affairs, out of fear and resistance we sometimes try to cut off the supply of one or more of these streams. We close off our minds, our hearts, or our energy supply and experience rigidity, cold-heartedness, or weakness or powerlessness. The Inner

Shaman continues to concentrate on the flow, but the flow is not acknowledged by the ego. This process of ignoring and shutting off access to the flow is the cause of all man-made suffering in the world. It is the source of all depression, anxiety, anger, greed, jealousy, envy, arrogance, stubbornness, impatience, victimization, self-destructiveness, and self-deprecation. These are all activities fostered by the false personality to keep us from identifying with the Inner Shaman, which is the death knell for the ego.

Eventually, after working with these three streams, you will begin to understand that your body is no more than the seed-pod, the container for the seed of who you are, which is absolute truth, infinite love, and boundless energy. This seedpod has a very important function and needs to be cared for and nourished, but when it is time for the seed to germinate, the seedpod opens and falls away revealing the real life within. This does not mean that you have to die to give birth to the seed; it simply means that you have to transfer your identification from your body personality to your true identity within your heart, the Inner Shaman, the seeds of creation—the gold seed of truth, the rose seed of love, and the electric blue seed of energy. These colors combined represent who you are; you no longer confuse who you are with the container that is temporarily holding them. These three streams are quantum, infinite, unlimited, and to be found everywhere, all though time, space, and beyond. As you identify with them, you begin to sense that you are unlimited and connected to the infinite source of power, love, and wisdom. When this realization becomes complete, you have achieved self-realization, *samadhi*, *satori*, enlightenment.

4

THE BENEFITS of WORKING
with the INNER SHAMAN

By now, I hope, you have begun to appreciate the importance and value of the Inner Shaman, and the integral part it plays in your ultimate happiness and fulfillment. As you work with the Inner Shaman, a variety of inner events will begin to take place. Here are some, but not all, of the transitions that will occur:

1. You will become less identified with your story.
2. You will become less identified with your body, but will be able to take better care of it than ever before.
3. You will be freed of some or all of the habits that caused you unhappiness, pain, and suffering.
4. You will recognize your agreements and be able to fulfill them better than ever.
5. You will recognize and resolve karmic commitments without resistance.

6. You will experience yourself to be much more at peace and feel much less victimized by your life experiences.
7. You will experience rapid results from your thoughts and actions.
8. You will experience more joy and satisfaction than ever before.
9. You will recognize and appreciate the beauty around you more than ever.
10. You will experience an amazing increase in your creativity and productivity.
11. You will experience yourself to be more intelligent and more knowledgeable than before.
12. You will be more neutral and accepting in the face of annoying people and life problems.
13. You will feel more detached from money, from obstacles, and from conditions you hitherto had required for your happiness.
14. You will feel more compassion for others and forgiveness for people you would formerly have judged.
15. Your understanding will be more global and more synergistic.
16. Your interactions with people will be more pleasurable, friendly, and respectful.
17. Animals will be more drawn to you.
18. You will have more energy and feel younger.
19. You will experience greater freedom in your dreaming and visions for what you want. There will be rapid results.
20. There will be exceptions to all of the above until you advance to mastery level.

As you become more experienced in working with the Inner Shaman, you will find yourself more in the driver's seat of your life. You will have more power to accomplish your aims and visions, so it is imperative that you are clear about what you want in your life. It will no longer suffice for you simply to react to events that appear to be happening to you. Rather, you will become increasingly aware that you are the author of your experiences—and your experiences are generated by the thoughts you choose to focus on. This is a very empowering idea—and you'll find that you rise to become more proactive in your life.

As you become empowered through your allegiance to the Inner Shaman, you will find it much more difficult to feel at the mercy of others, victimized by life circumstances, controlled by your habitual way of telling your story. You will discover that, in fact, the way you tell the story of your life changes. Rather than your story being one of pain and woe, ending in failure and disappointment, it will start to resemble the hero's journey, in which every challenge has brought you to a higher state of mastery and maturity.

You will feel wiser and more accepting, and your compassion will grow for others who are struggling through their ignorance. At the same time, you will find yourself becoming more ruthless, less willing to put up with your own whining because you will know for a fact that those feelings are not accurate and should not be tolerated. While you may be more compassionate overall you will simultaneously be less inclined to feel sorry for others who repeatedly moan and groan for the sake of attention.

EXERCISE **TELLING THE STORY OF YOUR LIFE**

You can do this exercise alone, by writing in a journal or computer, or with a partner, with whom you can exchange stories. It is eye-opening to listen to another's story and observe their reactions.

First, tell the story of your life, starting from your birth, as if you are a complete victim of circumstances. This story is a tragedy of difficult events that leads you to feel very sorry for yourself. Take as long as you wish, depending on the length of your life and how much detail you want to include.

Next, tell the same story, but this time you are a hero or heroine who transcends challenges and difficulties to emerge victorious. All those difficult events were tests or initiations, and each led to powerful lessons that accelerated your maturity. Notice the effect on your listener and/or on your own mood. Which story do you prefer? Which story is more true? Which story will be the official story you will tell from now on? Which story will you tell yourself? Are you ready to let go of your deep resentment or martyred feelings? Are you ready to release the pleasure of making others feel sorry for you? Are you ready for a new story?

BEYOND YOUR STORY

In the end, you don't need a story, because all stories are fiction anyway. Shamanically speaking, it does not matter what happened in the past, no matter how difficult or easy it was. What is important is what you are experiencing now and what you have concluded about what you think you've been through. That has everything to do with the quality of your presence and experience today.

I cannot emphasize enough the importance of this aspect of shamanism. I used to feel that it was important to tell the unvarnished truth about my past and not sugar-coat the story with idealistic claptrap or complete denial of what actually happened. However, it began to dawn on me that this emphasis on the truth was very subjective. How could I be trusted to know what the truth was when all my memories and attitudes were flavored with my own biases and opinions? I discovered that I did not know what the truth was; all the thoughts and feelings that came from my surface personality were suspect, because they were coming from my false personality, not from the Inner Shaman. How did I know that? Because any thoughts or feelings with an axe to grind, anything with a hidden agenda, is coming from the false personality.

Take a few minutes to think deeply about this. When you let it penetrate, you will see that it is revolutionary. The false personality has attitude. The Inner Shaman is neutral; it has no agenda. It does not care that you think you got whipped, abused, or beaten by life. All it says is, "Wake up, you have been having a bad dream. You are present and awake now, not limited by anything." The mind wants to protest and says, "Yes, but what about this and what about that?" There is anger, outrage, rebellion. All that is attitude and should be a red flag. The Inner Shaman is ruthless and only tells the truth; it is lovingly neutral, like a wise parent calming an upset and recalcitrant child.

5

HOW the INNER SHAMAN CAME to BE

Here is a mythic story that tells the tale of the Inner Shaman and how it came to be. Often stories and myths get to the truth better than dogma or other attempts to be empirical.

A long, long time ago, a time so long ago that time had not even been created yet, the Great Spirit, also known as the Tao, was enjoying just being the grand source of everything, and in the Great Spirit's musing about what was and what might be, Spirit looked around and said, "Wouldn't it be wonderful if I created a mini-me to share the universe with me? I will have a child." And with that thought a child was created, and that child instantly began to frolic and play and create—and, as children do, it imagined that it was many characters, playing them all at once. So instantly quadrillions of mini-mes formed, all facets and reflections of the Great Spirit who was both mother and father to all this activity. The Great Spirit had realized the dream of sharing all of creation. The mini-mes instantly began to marvel over their existence and their ability to enjoy being aware of everything. They played and frolicked with creation in an infinite moment of now, making their own experiences out of the Great Spirit's grand palette. (All those sparks of awareness are what we experience to be our individual selves.)

One cosmic day, we—the mini-mes—had an interesting new thought. It was a crazy, impossible thought, but nevertheless, in the infiniteness of everything, the thought had to come up somehow, some way. The thought was, "I wonder what it would be like to be in a universe where I am the creator of everything. What if I pretended that there was no Great Spirit but me?" Well, in the cosmos one cannot have an idle thought that is not instantly actualized and explored. So instantly there was dreamed up an illusory physical universe. Out of nothing, a physical universe was given birth—with the dimensions of time and space. The mini-mes were excited and helped suns and planets to develop that would sustain life. Dividing into seven rays, the mini-mes selected higher life forms to incarnate into, specializing into seven different types of sentient physical beings: artisans, sages, servers, priests, warriors, kings, and scholars. As soon as they did this, as per their creative idea, they completely (but temporarily) forgot their source and identified with the physical bodies they occupied.

Dimly, through the instinctive layers of their DNA, they remembered their creator, their source, so they built primitive idols and worshipped various imagined gods and feared their wrath, as they felt guilty about the experiment in imagined separation. Although they had not expected it, with physical life they experienced illness, pain, grief, fear, anger, and death. These unpleasant experiences were the by-products of the world they had dreamed up. They sought refuge in the many distractions of their dream, hoping that these dramas would help them to escape from their suffering. Their pain also motivated them to seek answers, to find relief from fear, doubt, and all manner of misery. Eventually, with time and evolution, they became philosophers and theologians trying to explain the situation; but, with regularity, the false personality clouded their perspective, which led to endless conflicts, persecutions, and wars. Confusion reigned supreme until a very few of them—the mystics, shamans, rishis, Zen masters, and adepts—through deep meditation and inward focus, broke through the mystery. When they did so, they laughed long and loud, tears of mirth running down their faces.

The rest of the people thought these enlightened ones were crazy, but they were not. For the first time ever, they were sane. They had discovered that the reality they had been so fixated on was nothing more than a dream, a complex hallucination created by a combination of amnesia and their most firmly held beliefs in limitation, entrapment, and separation. They finally realized that they had never left the Great Spirit, because that was impossible. The Great Spirit was and is everywhere at all times, completely available through the quantum connection of the DNA they had created. So they were only dreaming that they had left creation in order to explore that interesting but impossible thought, "separation." In amazement, they understood that they had never separated from Spirit. The grief, illness, hatred, fear, and death they thought were real were in fact never true. They had simply fallen asleep for a time and were having a dream that had become unpleasant. The unpleasantness of the dream was due to the ego, the false personality that they had made to pretend to dominate this experience and control it through denying Spirit, and exploiting the twin illusions of fear and separation.

They also realized that at the core of each one of them was an original spark of the Great Spirit, a facet of the same diamond, an Inner Shaman. Furthermore, they realized that this essence made each human an aspect of one undivided being. They learned that they were not separate mini-mes after all and that there was but one extraordinary child of the Great Spirit. Many of the great avatars, such as Jesus and Siddartha Gautama (who became the Buddha), discovered this, as did countless other mini-mes who finally remembered who they were, children of the Tao, of Christ and Buddha consciousness. This is the I Am, the Inner Shaman that you are being introduced to in this book, the one offspring of the source.

THE CONSEQUENCES FOR THE INNER SHAMAN

There is more to this story. For a long time, the mini-mes that woke up to the truth of the Inner Shaman were put to death or persecuted by the other mini-mes because they were upsetting the false dream. They were rocking the boat, so to speak. The enlightened ones either had to remain in hiding or had to couch their teachings in poetry or heavily disguised prose in order to remain undetected. Many shamans skipped written teachings altogether and taught about the Inner Shaman orally for generation after generation. This became the way of indigenous peoples. Eventually some enlightened ones, like the Hindu teacher Patanjali, were able to get their teachings out in written form and describe step by step how to break through and free the truth.

There is a further aspect to this story. Indigenous shamanic tribes around the world share a surprising understanding. From the Dogon of West Africa to the Australian Aboriginals, the Maoris of New Zealand, the Hawaiians of the Pacific, the Incas of South America and the Mayas in Central America, all believe that humans were seeded from a planet orbiting a sun in the Pleiades, which are also known as the Seven Sisters. In other words, they believe that when a people becomes advanced enough, their shamans go out and help life forms to evolve into sentient beings in new locations in the universe. So shamans believe that life can be found everywhere in this physical universe, and that advanced souls exist on other planets and have a hand in helping others who are just starting out elsewhere. Through their dreams, shamans visit locations beyond the earth and can describe in vivid detail what conditions are like there and the beings who inhabit them. These they refer to as the star nation or star people. Scientists have been amazed that the Dogon people, living without plumbing or electricity, have calculated the exact distances to various celestial bodies like the sun and the moon, as well as the exact distance to the Pleiades. When asked how they do it, their response is simply to say that they go to these places all the time.

Shamans are known for their ability to journey to various worlds to retrieve knowledge, to conduct soul retrievals, to find lost objects, to map the universe, and to communicate with life forms in other locations. The United States military has conducted longitudinal studies in remote viewing (modern terminology for ancient shamanic skills), the ability to see details of military installations in locations where they are unable to go physically. Retired military personnel have revealed to me that these studies have been successful and that the military relies on them. This type of research is now common knowledge and has been admitted to by various governments around the world, including that of Russia and our own.

EXERCISE **LEARNING TO NAVIGATE OUTSIDE THE BODY**

This is a shamanic training exercise to develop the ability to leave the body at will and perform specific tasks.

1. Lie down or sit in a chair. Close your eyes and take some deep breaths. Now slowly count down

from ten to one, breathing out slowly and relaxing your abdomen.

2. Picture one of the corners of the room up near the ceiling, if you are indoors. If outdoors, select a perch up in a branch of a tree or an exact location just above you.

3. Instantly imagine that you are there and looking around from that perspective. Look down and see your body below. Look around at the room or the land and identify what you see from that angle.

4. Now instantly go back into your body and notice how you entered your body. Through the top of your head? Through your heart? Through your solar plexus?

5. Go back up into your perch and take a look at your body again. See if you can see more than just your body from there—perhaps your energy field, or inside your body as well. What do you see?

6. Now go back and occupy your body again.

7. Continue to do this, changing perches and locations, each time looking around and checking things out. At first, always go back to your body in between changes.

8. Eventually you can shift from one perch to another without returning to your usual perspective in your body. You may also want to try more remote locations little by little.

EXERCISE **EXPANDING TO TRAVEL**
TO THE OUTER LIMITS OF THE UNIVERSE

The following is a training exercise to help shamans develop
expertise in the ability to travel great distances through space.

1. Lie down or sit in a chair, and be as comfortable
   as possible. Close your eyes and feel the force of
   gravity on your body. Notice how it pulls on your
   limbs and head and keeps you firmly on the floor
   or in your chair. Without it, you would simply float
   away. You can count on the fact that gravity will
   keep your body firmly parked while you are on your
   journey. You are perfectly safe where you are. Notice
   that your imagination is not confined by gravity.
   There you are free to go wherever you wish.

2. Now focus on your heart and imagine that this is
   the beginning of your journey. Imagine that your
   heart is filled with light and that this intense golden
   light begins to expand and you with it. It radiates
   outward to fill your entire body and then begins to
   radiate outside you to fill your whole luminous egg.

3. Quickly, it fills the whole room or space you are in.
   Expanding out, this intense golden light encompasses
   the whole building, then the whole neighborhood,
   then the whole town or city, and still continues to
   expand outward to include the entire region, county,
   state, and section of the country you are in.

4. Not stopping, this intense golden light radiates
   out to the whole country, then crosses borders
   into adjacent countries and fills them. You extend

beyond coastlines, occupying oceans and then other continents, rapidly filling up the whole world. The light expands upward into the atmosphere and then to the edge of space.

5. On it expands, toward the moon and the other planets and the sun, until it moves beyond the solar system. Quickly it crosses space to adjacent planetary systems with their suns and crosses the Milky Way.

6. After filling the entire Milky Way, this intense golden light extends in all directions toward other galaxies, swallowing them up, and moves farther and farther toward the outer reaches of space. Eventually it encounters unimaginable regions at the edge of space and continues beyond them to regions you have no knowledge of, and beyond them to limitless regions.

7. And now you take a big deep breath. You are huge, bigger than anything you can imagine. It is time to return. You call in your light and direct it to reverse direction. You begin to contract back inward.

8. Back the light zooms through the limitless regions, back through billions of galaxies, back through lengthy reaches of space, headed for your own galaxy, the Milky Way.

9. Back it comes, shrinking from the whole galaxy toward a tiny planetary system on one of the galaxy's arms. Suddenly you are back in this solar system

and, shrinking fast, you zoom past the planets and the sun, past the moon into the atmosphere of the beautiful blue-green earth.

10. Down you go through the atmosphere to the ground itself and the oceans, where you begin to recede back across continents and great bodies of water, back across countries, back across borders, into your own country, region, neighborhood, house, back into your room or yard, back toward that body of yours parked in a chair or on the ground . . .

11. And back into your energy field, back into your body, back to feeling your center in your heart. You are safely home, for the time being.

12. Relax, and take a big deep breath. Wiggle your fingers and toes. Thank gravity for keeping your body stable; open your eyes and you are back to this part of the dream you have been having. Done.

Do this often, and you will experience greater and greater ability to travel remotely outside of your body.

Today, only Western scientists are unclear about our status in the cosmos. From a shamanic standpoint, the question of whether humans are alone in the universe was answered long ago: sentient life exists across the galaxies, from one end of the universe to another. After all, why would the mini-mes choose to occupy only one tiny planet on the outskirts of a relatively small galaxy among billions? The simple answer is, they wouldn't.

6

LOCATING the INNER SHAMAN WITHIN YOU

The truth is, as you have seen, that the Inner Shaman has no exact location, because, like particles in the quantum field, it can be everywhere and anywhere in the universe at the same time. Shamanically speaking, in the dreamscape, we believe ourselves to be human, living on Earth in the early 2000s. Remember that shamans believe that we are consensually dreaming this reality and that it is not nearly as fixed or as stable as we think. Modern physicists are confirming these shamanic insights. This set of beliefs about what year it is and what planet this is form the current setting for the "assemblage point," a shamanic term for an organizing principle that assembles all the information from our quantum DNA and gives us a temporary identity, like a role an actor takes in a play. Keep in mind that shamans do not consider this play we call "being human" to be the only reality, but merely one of many probabilities. For the shaman, it is a temporary state that allows us to have physical experiences and learn lessons. For the shaman, it is a very real-seeming dream that may shift flexibly and accommodate our needs. To give you a simple example, recall a time when you lost your car keys and you looked everywhere, perhaps searched the car or your purse many times over. Then you came back a little later and there they were in an obvious place, which you had searched repeatedly already.

Since we are experiencing ourselves to be localized in our human bodies, it is practical to locate the Inner Shaman in the most accessible place. That place is as close as possible; as described in chapter 1, it is in the exact center of your chest, between top and bottom, front and back, and left and right, surrounded by the lungs. This is why the breath is related to Spirit in so many spiritual traditions. As you recall from chapter 3, the portal to the Spirit World, held within, is within the sino-atrial valve of the heart.

Therefore, the best way for you to contact the Inner Shaman is to focus on your physical heart. Go ahead and close your eyes for a moment, take a deep breath, and drop down inside your body to your chest. Sense your heart residing there, inside your ribcage, just behind and to the left side of your sternum. Find the part of the heart where you sense a special feeling, and this will become a sanctuary.

Recall that all the major mystical paths reference the heart as the power place and core location for awakening—not the cerebrum or brain. They teach that the path to God is the way of the heart. The Q'ero "walk the path of the heart," as do the Mayas, as do the Dine (Navajo), as do the Maori. The list of examples goes on. Remember that mystical Christianity shows Jesus, Mother Mary, and other saints pointing to their hearts as the key to Christian teachings. Catholics refer to this point within as the Sacred Heart, and it is featured in sculptures and paintings in cathedrals and churches all over the world. The synergy of these teachings is not accidental. When they point to the heart as the source of the path, they mean it literally.

Bear in mind that the importance of the path of the heart was known to shamans long before Christianity, Islam, or any of the major world religions. This suggests that what is true does not become lost but is rediscovered again and again in time. As long as people have had a heart, they have somehow known the power of it.

THE POWER OF THE HUMAN HEART

Your heart has a powerful magnetic field, much stronger than that of your brain. According to recent research conducted by Rollin McCraty, PhD, Director of Research at the Institute of HeartMath, the heart generates an electromagnetic field five hundred times more powerful than the brain's. In fact, it is the strongest rhythmic electromagnetic field in the body and can be detected by instruments several feet away from the body. McCraty and his fellow researchers believe that this field acts as a carrier wave for information from the heart, or in other words a synchronizing signal for the entire body, informing the body at an electromagnetic level just below conscious awareness. In addition, McCraty and his team found that the heart directly affects the amygdala, one of the most important emotional processing centers in the brain. The amygdala is associated with fight-or-flight responses, but what most people do not know is that it is also deeply related to the experience of ecstasy. So we now have scientific evidence that the heart—not just the brain—can stimulate the experience of ecstasy. What's more, scientists are learning that the heart is directly involved in the intuitive process. The data point to the fact that both the heart and the brain are able to receive information about future events before they happen, but the heart receives the information first. In fact, the heart has been reclassified as an endocrine gland after the discovery that it secretes a special hormone called ATF (atrial natriuretic factor) that affects the adrenals, blood vessels, kidneys, and large parts of the regulatory system of the brain. The heart also secretes oxytocin—the so-called "love hormone" related to childbirth, cognition, adaptation, tolerance, bonding, and complex sexual and maternal activities. Finally, the heart has been shown to affect the coherence of the cortical functions in the brain through neural information pathways. When the heart rhythm patterns are coherent, people experience positive feelings, mental clarity, more creativity, and improved decision-making abilities.

Your heart is like the sun in that it radiates light and energy throughout your body and beyond, and magnetizes to itself energetically what you need. And according to many mystical traditions, your heart is the bridge between the sun and the earth as it communicates with both of them, assisting you in being both coherent as a biological organism and in tune with your environment.

There is no doubt that your heart is the center, the key place of power in your body, and your path to the riches of the Inner Shaman. So you can see how important it is to be in communication with your heart and to keep it metaphorically open and accessible. This translates into a healthy heart. If your heart is closed, you will have difficulty being healthy and coherent as a human being—and this is the cause of much illness, despair, and anxiety. Over half a million Americans die of heart disease every year. In the United States, heart attacks are the leading cause of death for both men and women, being responsible for one in every four deaths. Approximately 715,000 Americans have heart attacks every year, and the cost of this is about $109 billion a year. One could say that all this illness is the result of diet, but it is way more than that. The relatively new international index of environmental sustainability and well-being ranks the United States in the lowest category for happiness. Despite their freedoms and high standard of living, Americans are not a happy people compared with their neighbors in the world. The health data reflects it.

EXERCISE **RADIATING LIGHT FROM THE HEART**

1. Take a moment right now to focus on your heart. Feel the warmth there and the sensations of aliveness it holds.

2. Allow yourself to feel grateful for whatever gifts have come your way, whatever you fully appreciate about your life. Take your time here.

3. Now imagine that your heart is filling with the most sublime golden light from within. Imagine the light becoming brighter and brighter, shining like the sun. Now your heart is glowing so bright that you may find it hard to look at, just like the sun.

4. Notice how the feeling in your heart strengthens and the light spreads outward to the trillions of cells in your body, feeding and nurturing them, filling them up with what they crave, golden light: balancing, refining, healing, vitalizing, and renewing.

5. When your body is completely full of light, let this brilliance radiate outward through your pores to fill up the luminous egg around you and beyond.

6. Fill the entire room, or your entire space, with the golden light. Pay attention to the slightest nuances

of change you begin to experience. What do you feel? What are the sensations? How does this affect your outlook and perception?

7. Now draw back all this light inside your skin and imagine closing off your pores to keep it within.

This is the domain of the Inner Shaman.

HOW THE INNER SHAMAN APPEARS

You have seen how your Inner Shaman keeps constant vigil over you within the space of your heart, but what might that Inner Shaman look like in your mind's eye? As you will soon see, it may look like almost anything, but it is good to have a sense of what shamans look like in the real world. These days, most shamans dress in Western-style clothes unless they are performing a ritual or ceremony. This is because most shamans have regular jobs in addition to providing shamanic service to their communities. They may be fishermen or farmers; they may work for the railroad or the post office, drive cabs, care for children, teach in school, or prepare food in restaurants. I have met shamans with many different kinds of day jobs. Let us focus here on what shamans might look like when they are doing a shaman's work.

My teacher Guadalupe was a Huichol from Mexico, and he usually wore his native dress when doing any kind of ceremonial work, including healings. This consisted of a light cotton shirt with a colored neckerchief and pants, both white with highly colored embroidered thread forming designs of deer, corn, lightning, and other symbols. He wore a broad-brimmed straw hat with a large peyote symbol on top made out of yarn and several vulture feathers stuck into the band. Around the brim were many little triangles dangling down that would shake with his every movement. On his brown, leathery feet he wore blue and white sandals with no socks. His native clothes were very beautiful and he attracted attention wherever he went in the United States. The Huichol women wear brightly colored skirts and blouses with scarves on their heads.

On the other hand, my male Shipibo teachers from the Amazon jungle wear a cotton robe with intricate designs embroidered all over it, designs that represented song patterns for protection, while doing ceremony. The women shamans wear brightly colored blouses and a wraparound short skirt with similar designs to those on the men's robes. During ceremony, both wear a headband with more intricate designs and beads hanging down, and often a parrot feather or three sticking up in the front. They almost always carry a rattle made out of seedpods with designs similar to those on their clothing.

Andean shamans most often wear a wool poncho and a wool hat with earflaps to protect against the constant cold. Sometimes, as with the Q'ero, the wool hat is highly decorated with beads and other dangly ornaments. They are also fond of wearing short pants that end just below the knee. The women wear many layers of broad skirts and woolen sweaters. They wear many different types of colorful hats depending on their tribe.

Classic Siberian or Nepalese shamans, coming from a cold environment, wear layers of reindeer hide, with many necklaces as well as strings of bells that tinkle as they move. They often wear a face mask that hangs over their eyes, obscuring their vision. I have seen these face masks on Pomo Indian shamans in California as well, although they tend to wear robes made up entirely of turkey or redtail hawk feathers.

In very hot climates, such as the Kalahari desert of Africa, shamans may wear very little, just a loincloth and not much else. Most Native American shamans I have worked with wear a colored shirt or blouse and blue jeans, and the men will often wear cowboy boots, although I have also seen both men and women wear beaded moccasins. They will often wear a woolen ceremonial blanket or scarf with colors and designs that have significance for them. During ceremony they carry eagle, hawk, or parrot-feather fans. They too use rattles and drums, sometimes large ones designed for many people to drum on at once, as in powwows and sundances.

Your Inner Shaman, too, may take on a wide variety of appearances. Let us talk a little about how to see before doing an exercise to meet the Inner Shaman within ourselves.

THE ART OF INNER SEEING

Now that you have been introduced to the power and importance of the heart from both a Western medical perspective and the shamanic perspective, we will link it to that other important seat of consciousness, the third eye, the spot just above the nose and between the eyebrows. For shamans, the two most important places of "seeing" are the heart and the brow; they work together for optimal "knowing." If you can keep your attention on these two places simultaneously, the pace at which your shamanic skills develop will accelerate rapidly. Remember that shamans are known for having a foot in two worlds simultaneously; this is a good example of how they do that.

Both the heart and the third eye are related to inspiration, the ability to lift up to higher frequencies of perceiving and understanding. Ignore these centers, and it is difficult to perceive anything other than the surface appearance of a very conventional world. It is a little like seeing only the paint job when looking at a car you are thinking of buying. It won't tell you much about what is on the inside, and it would be a foolish way to approach the task; you are likely to end up with a car in poor mechanical condition. By opening up your vision, you can penetrate beyond appearance, and this will make you much more effective in everyday life. This is a skill you can develop with practice, as all human beings come equipped with the hardware to see below the surface.

EXERCISE **SEEING FROM THE HEART AND THE THIRD EYE**

Here we are going to cultivate the art of inner seeing or sensing, the ability to perceive dimensions not seen by the naked eye or heard by external hearing. This is done best by concentrating on a space just behind the bridge of your nose and between your eyes, about two to three inches into your skull. Taoist shamans have called this place the yintang or Lotus Flower, a location that allows one to stop time, to be in a place of great silence and peace.

1. Imagine there is a little room in the yintang, where you can sit in an armchair and contemplate whatever you want. Take several minutes to relax and breathe evenly, thinking of nothing in particular. With each exhale, relax your body more deeply. This will change your brain state and shift you from beta or ordinary brainwaves to alpha or theta brainwaves, highly conducive to viewing, hearing, and feeling inner states.

2. When you are ready, turn your attention down toward your heart. You may find yourself actually dropping down and experiencing yourself from that level of your body.

3. Next, in the space of your physical heart, imagine a little room and in the middle of that room see, sense, or feel a special seat, a shaman's chair or throne, like the kind that shamans around the world

use to practice healing or perform ceremonies. If you prefer, the seat may be a simple cushion, like those used by Zen masters in deep meditation.

4. On this seat, imagine, sense, or feel a powerful radiating figure, the Inner Shaman, glowing with a golden crystalline light. He or she may be dressed indigenously in the raiment of shamans from varying traditions.

- The shaman's head will most likely be encircled by a corona, a highly decorated beaded band that enhances the mind and offers protection. There may be eagle, hawk, or parrot feathers, or perhaps a headdress that includes other types of decoration, such as a crown or tiara. It may have strands of cloth, leather, or beads hanging down over the face.

- The shaman may be wearing a robe, a *kushma* (a Shipibo robe with song patterns), furs, a shawl, a poncho, or nothing at all on the upper part of the body. The robe or shawl may be artistically decorated with meaningful patterns and designs representing prayers and songs.

- The lower body may be clothed in leggings, covered by the robe, or bare, as in the case with shamans from the tropics and equatorial zones.

- There may be tattoos, necklaces, earrings, finger rings, bracelets, or anklets. On the shaman's feet may be moccasins, boots, or sandals, or they may be bare. The shaman may be holding a staff, a healing wand, a rattle, a drum, a scepter, a crystal, a feather fan, a wing, or a single beaded feather.

- In some cases the Inner Shaman will take the form of a known deity or a divine figure who may be important to you, such as Quan Yin, Isis, the Virgin Mary, the Virgin of Guadalupe, Jesus, Buddha, Yogananda, Ganesh, Wiracocha, or Krishna. The Inner Shaman might look like Mickey Mouse, a superhero, Merlin, Glenda the Good from Oz, Wonder Woman, Kali, or perhaps a totem animal. Don't be too concerned about how this Inner Shaman shows up, or if the figure changes over time. These trappings are less important than the impact the Inner Shaman has upon you. In other words, don't get attached to the form; just enjoy and appreciate the presence, and be grateful that you have such a powerful resource as close to you as anyone could ever get.

- This shaman that you see or feel within is your Inner Shaman. His or her eyes may be closed in deep meditation or open, revealing depth, experience, loving-kindness, and wisdom. They will be clear and penetrating but not intrusive. There will be humor there as well as compassion.

- On occasion you may find the Inner Shaman not sitting but dancing, drumming, rattling, standing, blessing with arms outstretched, holding mudras (hand positions), making an offering, or singing. Anything is possible; do not judge what comes to you. With experience you may develop some understanding of what the Inner Shaman is communicating to you via the various ways it shows up. In my experience, every nuance of the Inner Shaman is meaningful.

5. Mentally voice your appreciation to the Inner Shaman for maintaining a constant vigil within you, for considering you so important that he or she is willing to be with you every second of every day and night throughout your whole life.

THE LIGHT OF THE INNER SHAMAN

No matter how the Inner Shaman appears to you, the key ingredient is light. The Inner Shaman radiates the most beautiful clear, crystalline light, so bright it may be difficult to look at. You may find that the shaman's form dissolves into pure light and you can discern the figure no more. For shamans, light is the truest form of everything in the physical world, including human beings. They say that at the most fundamental level, everything is light. Certainly the Spirit World is filled with light and so, naturally, as one penetrates to the deeper levels of reality, all forms become pure light.

You may find that the Inner Shaman appears more like a brilliant diamond, crystal, or gemstone filled with light. Not only is this perception very beautiful, but it is quite common and a sign that you are seeing more deeply than surface reality. Whatever the case, accept whatever you experience and regard it as all good.

In addition to the visible appearance of the Inner Shaman, you may experience an extraordinary warmth or tingling in your chest, a glowing and radiating sensation that feels both powerful and expansive. Enjoy the sensation to the utmost. On occasion, you may experience some fearfulness, and perhaps think you are having heart palpitations that may induce a heart attack. Do not pay heed to such fears, as these are forms of resistance to you accelerating and moving toward inner power. The ego or false personality does not like you to pay attention to the Inner Shaman and will always attempt to distract you with thoughts that lead you away from the experience. If these random worries or concerns persist, focus for a time on your breathing. Breathing in, think the word "accepting." Breathing out through the top of your head and shoulders, think the word "releasing." In this way you will make whatever form of resistance is arising disappear, and will be able to return to contemplating the Inner Shaman. Stay with this as long as you like. Another method of dealing with resistance is to focus on the distracting thought for a moment while stating unequivocally, "You have no power over me." It will release soon enough.

You might also meet your inner skeptic. You might say, "Well, this is just all in my imagination. I'm making it all up. There is no Inner Shaman really. This whole thing is bogus." I would then say to you that you are both right and very wrong. Of course you are using your imagination. That is the principal vehicle by which you can perceive powerful inner states and experiences. You use your imagination to recall memories in the same way. You have to use the right tool for the job, and your imagination is the tool. How else would you perceive the Inner Shaman—with your logic? It is not logical, so logic would be the wrong tool. With regard to making it up, everything you experience is made up, including the chair you are sitting in. You think there is an objective reality, but there is not. As you may recall from our discussion earlier, quantum physics tells us that. Every mystic will tell you that as well. The chair you are sitting in is hardly there; it is made up of particles winking in and out of form, made up through agreed-upon beliefs that it is there, but that doesn't mean it is bogus. You will discover that the Inner Shaman is perhaps the most real thing in your universe because it is the royal doorway to true reality, rather than the external world we think of as reality.

This leads us to one of the core shamanic teachings. Never accept appearances. Appearances too often lie to us. Any form that the Inner Shaman takes is largely symbolic. It has no real form or objective shape. Rather, it is a state of being, a state of pure consciousness and awareness. Remember that symbols are the language of the Spirit World, what many people call the subconscious or the higher realms. Don't mistake the symbol for the real thing.

7

WHAT SHAMANS
KNOW about the MIND

Psychologists and social scientists know that conditioning and behavioral patterns guide the way the observable mind works. Our thoughts are, to some degree, programmed; they operate by stimulus response. Shamans have always been astute psychologists and counselors, since understanding themselves and others allows them to be of greater service. Through the ages, they have delved deeply into the mechanisms that humans employ to create illusions, delusions, denial, coping mechanisms, projections, rewards, and reinforcements. Shamans, however, go beyond modern-day psychology, since they have removed the artificial retaining walls in their own minds.

The way shamans see it, thoughts are things. These things can be focused on and, with intent, sent out to manifest something. Shamans say that at any given time there are clusters of thoughts, grouped together by similarity (because, with thoughts as with everything else, like attracts like), floating around looking for a place that resonates with them. These thoughts have been generated by billions of people over thousands of generations and are waiting to find a home in a living person's local thought system. Most of these thoughts are generated by the false personality, the parasite that dominates this particular dreamscape that we call reality. These are thoughts of separation, alienation, fear, attack, misery, and the like. Their purpose is to keep the human race divided at every turn, so that the dream of the parasite to master can prevail and thus the ongoing dream of a physical universe can continue.

The Shipibo people of the Upper Amazon are very careful to screen out, with tobacco and prayers, wandering thought forms that may come from unfriendly sources, even other shamans who might be mischievously trying to disrupt the effectiveness of their ceremony. In the Amazon, where there are fewer people, it is easier to feel the effects of negative thoughts wandering around. Many shamans around the world have become experts in the ability to remove darts, little projectiles sent by negative shamans through intense focus to do harm in their victims. Negative shamans, usually known as sorcerers, may be hired by clients to create illness in order to get rid of a competitor in love or to obtain revenge for a perceived wrong. Negative shamans exist wherever shamanism is practiced, because there are criminal types in every profession, especially where power can be abused. These dangerous shamans train by focusing closely on little twigs up in a tree. They repeatedly send thoughts of projectiles at these twigs until they succeed in breaking one with a thought, an intention. You can imagine what they can do to a human body. They become powerful directors of thought forms.

Shamans also believe that nothing is random in the universe; everything happens for a purpose. Our childhood experiences are not accidental, nor are the parents who programmed us with specific beliefs, nor are the circumstances of our birth and early years. According to shamanic thinking, our essence chose these circumstances in order to learn lessons. Eventually the false personality tries to manipulate these circumstances to its own advantage, and under this divisive influence we allow circumstances to program us in ways that attract thoughts and feelings that establish and reinforce retaining walls in the mind. We either labor under the limitations of these beliefs and suffer terribly, or we become aware of the walls and set about finding the power to tear them down.

We are programmed to believe that events impact us in such a way as to make us react with thoughts and feelings. Something makes us sad, something makes us angry, something makes us anxious, and so on. Shamans know that there is nothing actually out there to create these reactions; there are only projections of the mind. What passes for reality is actually a big screen that reflects back to us what we believe to be true. And what we believe is created by the ageless floating thoughts and feelings of the universal false personality, the parasite—thoughts and feelings that we attracted to ourselves and then played out, thinking they were ours. So, it is futile to try to change anything by manipulating events and objects in the projected world. That is like trying to change the outcome of a film by sticking a hand in front of the projector or messing with the screen or shouting at the actors. The only solution is to look very closely and deconstruct the whole operation with astute observation, nonjudgment, and complete relaxation, and then ask for help from Spirit.

Again we are reminded of the basic shamanic dictum, "Never accept appearances." Nothing is actually as it seems. To be free, we must look beyond appearances, beyond assumptions, beyond our identifications. This is the most effective method of tearing down the retaining walls of the mind. This is the method that is tried and true for shamans, yet with focus and attention, anyone can do it. Remember to ask Spirit for help before doing this exercise.

EXERCISE RECAPITULATION: NOT DOING
AND STOPPING THE WORLD

1. Take any event or circumstance that is causing you trouble or unhappiness. Go over it in great detail. You can write it out if you wish: "First this happened and next I felt this way and then I did something that caused them to do that and then this happened," etc. Be specific in these details. Be clear about all the causes and effects that you believe to be the reason for the problem.

2. Notice the feelings this process generates. Make sure to write down the various feelings that seem to happen at each stage of the story.

3. Examine these feelings. Do not do anything about them. Take no action! This is about observation only. Focus on the first feeling and let yourself feel it exactly the way it shows up, without attempting to run away from it or resisting it in any way even if that's what you want to do. Stay with the feeling but don't magnify it or indulge in it. Do not judge it as good or bad. Relax your belly completely. Do not react; just observe the feeling and sensations of the body accompanying it.

Be aware of the feeling and let it flow without thinking other thoughts. The way the mind escapes from itself is to move from a feeling to a thought and then another one and then on to some action.

Thus the feeling is never actually experienced but is simply used as a springboard for other thoughts, feelings, and actions. Before you know it, you have a giant mess created by the false personality. This is what passes for life.

4. Experience your feeling to the fullest by simply observing it. Notice that while it seems to be related to a cause you have identified, it actually has a life of its own. You do not need a cause to have a feeling.

5. Next, look more closely at the possibility that this feeling may have resulted in the event that you thought was the cause of it. The feeling was there all along, which led to an event that verified the feeling. Sadness created a sad event. Anger created an event that you thought made you feel angry. The confusion comes from attaching the feeling to something. Notice that the feeling was there all along, just underneath your consciousness, but you didn't feel it until it created something in your experience that made you aware of it. If you had not had the feeling first, you would not have experienced the event. Your mind will want to argue with this vehemently. Be patient and just tell it, "Thank you for sharing."

   If something makes you angry, you can be sure you have been carrying anger. If something makes you anxious, you can be sure that you were already anxious. If a car almost runs you off the road, that is not the cause of your anxiety; it is a manifestation of the anxiety you were already carrying. The feeling is mechanical and programmed. It came from your imprinting, your early life experiences, traumas, resistances, and anything you brought with you into this life that is stored in your instinctive center, your DNA, and is drawn from the inventory of emotions generated by the ego.

6. As you experience the emotion in full, it will gradually diminish until it vanishes. It is thereby erased, and you have freed yourself of yet another impediment to your freedom. Even though you have freed yourself from this feeling in this moment, you may have other moments when you feel angry, or anxious, or whatever the feeling is, and the identical process will erase them. This takes time— and the false personality, being impatient and undisciplined, won't want to stay with this process.

The purpose of this exercise is to enable you to get rid of resistance to what you are feeling. It takes practice. When the resistance goes, the feelings that generate experience vanish and you become free.

Remember that the Inner Shaman is not content-oriented, nor does it experience ordinary emotions. These are activities of the false personality: rationalizations, projections, denials, and so on. The Inner Shaman is primarily engaged in higher-centered activities that lead to awe, joy, and bliss. The exercise above is designed to clear you of ordinary thoughts and emotions that are cluttering up the system, so that essence may shine through.

FINDING THE INFINITE MOMENT OF NOW

When you have learned to separate your feelings from your assumptions about what caused them, when you have learned not to resist your feelings and to surrender to what is, then you are ready to be more present. Here we will focus on the best method for finding the infinite moment of now, even as you navigate what seems to be linear time.

As you have seen, the Inner Shaman, largely ignored for centuries, can be discovered in the most obvious place, right within your heart. While the Inner Shaman is free to wander the universe, it is not free to take over your physical life because it respects and honors your free choice. The choice to keep the Inner Shaman trapped in its heart cave, mostly ignored, and to allow ego to steer your life course always results in suffering. It is not the route to joy and satisfaction. This does not mean that doing so is bad, because shamans do not judge choices as morally good or bad, but merely unfortunate if they lead to unpleasant consequences. The good news is that freeing the Inner Shaman, sooner or later, is inevitable, because it is the direction the river of the Tao is going. Every great spiritual teacher has said repeatedly that life's greatest purpose is to free the trapped essence and remove the false personality from its stranglehold on every detail of physical life. *A Course in Miracles* summarizes this teaching wonderfully when it says, "I am not the body. I am free. I am as God created me." Another way of saying this is, "I am not the parasite. I am the Inner Shaman and I am free. I am as expansive as Spirit originally created me to be. Nothing has actually changed from that plan."

As we have discussed, to liberate the Inner Shaman is to shift from identification with concrete, limited, physical "me" to "the context of me." What this means is: "When I am identified with concrete me, I am a small person against the world dealing with other people, other objects, outside events all happening to me. When I am the context of it all, I am the larger container, the stage that holds the actors, the props, all the events happening on that stage. If I am the context, nothing happens that is not me. The other actors are within me. They can't do anything to me because we are all one. This drama we seem to be experiencing is happening within me, not *to* me. As context I am infinitely more powerful, infinitely more compassionate, and vastly more understanding." The Inner Shaman is the whole context, is expansive, is indestructible, and is extraordinarily wise. To tap into these qualities, the Inner Shaman must be set free from its little cave of obscurity and brought out into mainstream light.

The essence becomes trapped in the illusion of time. We are often engaged in hallucinating the future or remembering what we think of as the past, but there is no power in this. The power is in the exact moment of the present, a moment so fleeting that it is no time at all. The false personality often flees to past and future and, even when noticing the present, resists it out of fear. The result is disengagement from the Inner Shaman, who is always present, no matter what, riding the limitless, tiny moments of now without thought and concern.

Only the Inner Shaman is able to maintain responsibility, to be engaged, to be present. The false personality flees from responsibility and becomes hopelessly entangled in the dream. The false personality is reactionary, victimized, martyred, and totally irresponsible. Not only is it unable to respond to the present moment, it is unable to experience itself as being in the driver's seat of the body. The net result is ongoing unredeemable suffering.

A few years ago, I was returning from my annual pilgrimage to visit the Huichol in central Mexico. I was asleep in the backseat when the car faltered and stopped. We had run out of gas in the Sonoran desert. It was decided that I should hitchhike to the nearest town, about twenty miles back. It was early afternoon and hot, so I was wearing only sandals, shorts, and a T-shirt. I was immediately picked up by a car traveling at a high rate of speed. In no time I got to the town, secured a container, bought a gallon of gas and thumbed a ride on a truck going north, back to where I had left the car and my family.

Unbeknownst to me, a car had stopped and given my group some gas, and they were speeding south to catch up with me. When I got back to where I'd left the car, it was gone and no one was there. The truck driver refused to let me off there, saying it was very dangerous for me to be alone in the desert, especially with all the drug problems. So now I was separated from my family and heading north in a truck with an uncertain destination. I had about twenty-five dollars in my wallet, and fortunately I was carrying my passport. Even so, a feeling of dread and panic began to set in. I was terribly worried about my family and their concern over me being missing, and also about how I was going to get home to Santa Fe. At that moment I was a victim of fate and events were happening to me.

Eventually the truck driver let me off at the passport control booth about forty miles from the US border, since he was turning off there. Now I was on my own, the sun was going down, it was getting cold, and I had no ride. I began to knock on car windows but no one would pick me up; I looked like a wild man, unshaven, with bloodshot eyes, and dressed in ratty clothes. I kept looking for my family, but they never turned up. Eventually I got a ride with a Mexican couple and an infant. They took me part way to the border, but I had to walk through Juarez at night, drug cartels and all.

Gradually I began to get control of myself and realized I was having a grand adventure arranged by my essence as a kind of test, or initiation, to see whether I would be a victim or the master of my destiny. I began to smile and relax as I recognized that all the characters in this adventure were parts of myself and that this was not happening to me but for me. I was perfectly safe as long as I knew I was. I was only unsafe when I viewed things as the enemy.

I got to the border and crossed, bought a windbreaker to stay warm and a couple of nutrition bars to feed myself, and called home to leave a message that I was all right and would take a bus home. I found the bus station and had just enough money to book a ticket for Santa Fe, a five-hour trip in the middle of the night. On the way it began to snow and I just shook my head and laughed some more looking out at the snowflakes. When I got to Santa Fe, my family was waiting to pick me up. They had had their own adventures, but that is another story. Everyone was tested to the limit; no one was a victim and we all passed the test.

The mini-me can become trapped in a nightmare of its own making when it feels disconnected, when the false personality cannot function adequately in the dream it made up. Eventually, everyone makes the discovery that life can only be successfully navigated when the Inner Shaman is in charge, and everyone resists the message until they are forced to accept it as true. What a game! Since the false personality hates surrender, it regularly arranges for the body to get beat-up badly and offers only a little pleasure in between.

The Inner Shaman is responsive because it is present and aware. When you are aware, you don't feel victimized. You see where you are going. You can be responsible for your experience because you don't feel separate from it. Here is a great and ancient exercise for learning to become totally present. Remember that this is the condition for the Inner Shaman to awaken.

EXERCISE **LEARNING TO RIDE THE TINY MOMENTS OF NOW**

Sit comfortably with arms and legs uncrossed. Become aware of your surroundings and your present state. Notice the present moment as best you can. Soon you will feel that you are riding the present moment, like a surfer on a wave, but the present moment may still feel messy because it is going by so fast. So divide the present moment into two parts. Still too messy? Cut it in half again, and then again. Keep cutting the present moment in half until it becomes extremely short, like maybe a millionth of a second, even smaller. Ride this teeny tiny moment of now.

This is still not maximally effective. Consider that when you get down to these tiny fragments of now, they are a done deal. There is nothing you can do to alter them in any way. All you can do is surrender to them, because they are going by so fast you cannot stop them and change them. They are, in a word, inevitable. When you live at this ever-present stream of tiny now points, all you can do is accept the inevitability of what is happening. You can resist all you want, but it is not going to make a damn bit of difference; all your resistance does is make the present moment into a negative experience, which can be defined as suffering. The now points are so short that they are like a series of snapshots. Absolutely nothing is going on. There is nothing to be done with these snapshots. They are fixed, like the thousands of still frames that make up a movie. Relax, surrender, and enjoy the view.

I suggest that you practice this often, for periods of one minute, two minutes, or five minutes. Work up to longer sequences of now points. You can do this several times a day. The more you practice, the more you will awaken the Inner Shaman and the more enlightened you will become.

8

TEARING DOWN
the RETAINING WALLS
of the MIND

T he retaining walls of the mind are nothing more than the strong, agreed-upon, and long-standing belief systems we hold. These thought systems are composed of social, cultural, and familial conditioning, which together form beliefs about your world. Typically these thought systems control you so that you behave in accordance with the expectations of those around you. Most of us are programmed to behave so that others will be able to control us, or at least so that others will feel comfortable around us. These thought systems generate emotions that motivate you to make choices. The choices you make lead you to take actions that generate consequences that usually reinforce your conditioned thought system. In this way, the retaining walls of your mind are reinforced over time, until you make the choice to dismantle them.

Let's say you grow up in a small town as a lower-class female. Early in life you learn that you have low social status and cannot expect to succeed economically the way those in the upper-crust culture do. Although you do well in school, you do not apply for college or scholarships because you don't feel important enough and don't believe you will succeed. This attitude causes no ripples or discomfort in your family, because you are fulfilling the expectations of your subculture. The choice to go to work at a low-level job leads to further choices that keep you limited, stuck in a life without many prospects. In this way, the culture at large keeps you in your lowly place and you do nothing to break the generational trend.

These thought systems persist because they are unexamined. In other words, the most successful and longest-lasting beliefs are those that remain beneath conscious awareness. Each of us has thousands of these programmed beliefs in our subconscious. Almost all of them are designed to limit the infinite amount of knowledge in the universe from pouring into us. Becoming aware of this fact for the first time and realizing the enormity of it can be truly devastating because it seems too big to escape from or fix. Confronting this reality is a tough initiation on the shamanic path, but there is a way out.

ANOMALIES THAT GIVE US A GLIMPSE OF OUR POWER AND FREEDOM

There have always been "exceptional" people—geniuses, idiot savants, and the like—who demonstrate extraordinary abilities. There are children who exhibit knowledge of foreign languages even though they have never been exposed to them. There are people who know their way around cities or landscapes that they have never visited in this life. There are blind people who can navigate perfectly. There are people who can calculate vast sums in the blink of an eye, faster than a computer. There are people who know about events that are about to take place, events far in the future, or precise details about your past that no stranger could know. There are people with severely damaged brains who have encyclopedic knowledge of things they have never studied, such as music or electricity.

How can this be? It seems that the universe is ready to pour knowledge into us. These people with exceptional abilities have escaped programming by some means or another and are still open to the logos, the knowledge of the universe. The DNA has a memory not unlike a vast computer, and is capable of holding almost limitless information, which it receives by induction from the overlapping energy fields everywhere in the universe.

I once spoke to a CIA operative who had participated in remote viewing experiments. He was able to see exact details of missile sites and other targets thousands of miles away. The experiments were anything but failures, but according to him, they were discontinued because they were not 100 percent accurate, 100 percent of the time. Shamans have used these abilities for thousands of years because they are not trained to ignore them or believe they don't have them. Your Inner Shaman is capable of remote viewing as well; you just haven't developed the skill yet.

Mainstream culture usually ignores these embarrassing exceptions because they don't fit the mold. We could conclude they are miracles so we don't have to explain them, but that would not be exactly true. They are not so much miracles as natural human abilities that are not developed or utilized by most people because of the cultural retaining walls in the mind. These are the abilities of the Inner Shaman in everyone.

I once had lunch with the man who held the Guinness record as the strongest man in the world. He was Icelandic, and he had managed to move several automobiles and a truck chained together by pulling on a rope with his little finger. When I met him at a conference for psychics in Denmark, I discovered that he could do other supernatural things. I watched as he lifted two large men up in each arm and then danced on flaming broken glass in his bare feet. I watched as he balanced his whole body by positioning his abdomen on the needle-sharp point of a steel knife. I watched as he magnetized his bare body to hold pieces of metal of all kinds, including pans, irons, forks, spoons, paper clips. In an act of intention he let go, and everything crashed to the ground. As I lunched with him after the demonstration, he told me that as a child living on a farm in isolated northern Iceland, he was not taught that people could not do certain things. One day when he was about ten years old, he fell off his uncle's tractor and it rolled over him, causing a terrible wound on his leg. Since he didn't know he could not do it, he simply willed the bleeding to stop. The wound closed up and he continued plowing the field. He went home without incident, without any trip to the doctor.

I can assure you that this man was very ordinary. His body was flesh and blood. He was not even very large—just a stout Icelandic man with a humble bearing. He was calm and serene, without guile. Yet his mind did work differently from those of most people. Because he did not have retaining walls in his mind that said he couldn't do things, the knowledge of the universe could pour into him. His Inner Shaman was completely accessible to him. Rather than thinking him amazing, I went away thinking that if he could do this, so could I if I just cleared away the retaining walls in my own mind.

CLEARING OUT THE SUBCONSCIOUS MIND

I learned from my shaman teachers that to clear the entire subconscious mind of all the mental constructs and belief systems of hundreds of lifetimes, and all the baggage, miasmas, and centuries' worth of garbage collected in the DNA, is an almost impossible task. To attempt this alone is not only extremely discouraging and time-consuming (meaning whole lifetimes of work), but unrealistic. The job cannot be done alone. The key to clearance is to ask for help, especially from Spirit, and from knowledgeable teachers. This is done most effectively by accessing your Inner Shaman. When you ask the Inner Shaman for help in purifying your DNA and clearing your subconscious mind of baggage, you will receive instantaneous help. Ask and you shall receive.

EXERCISE **CLEARING THE SUBCONSCIOUS MIND**

1. Sit and relax, taking several deep breaths. You will be giving clear commands to your subconscious, so it helps to be as relaxed as you can be.

2. Focus on the pull of gravity over your whole body. Feel how it makes you heavy. Allow gravity to do what it does to your body with no resistance.

3. Shift your attention to your imagination and to your mind, where gravity has no pull whatsoever.

4. Now imagine that you are entering an elevator, and that you are going to go down from the tenth floor to the ground floor. Feel the elevator lurch and begin to go down: ten, nine, eight, relaxing, going deeper, seven, six, five, letting go, relaxing even more, four, three, going down, two, one, deeply relaxed and ready.

5. Let the door to the elevator open and step out into a natural landscape of great beauty. Before you is a wise old man or woman, smiling and beckoning you to come nearer.

6. Say to this wise person: "Thank you for being here. I came to ask you for help with clearing my subconscious mind of all extraneous baggage and limitations that are holding me back from growing and transforming. I know you can and will do this because I am using my free will to ask for your services. Begin to dismantle all retaining walls in my mind that are holding me back at this time. As I breathe each breath, the retaining walls fall away along with thousands of years of programming, worry, fears, and self-deprecation, including self-imposed blocks due to guilt and shame. Remove all guilt, all shame, all lack of forgiveness. Remove all anger, vengefulness, grief, and remorse. I no longer need any of these things for my progress forward."

7. Now say: "I am already feeling lighter, freer, transformed into my essence self. Thank you, thank you for helping me even when I am not consciously aware of it. From now on, you and I are partners. I know you want me to be ultimately successful in this endeavor and I will not resist or fight your efforts to assist me. I am that I am. I am the open door that no man can shut. I am on my way."

8. Now return to the elevator, enter, and close the door. Push the button and begin to rise up one, two, three, feeling lighter and more focused, four, five, six, clearer and more in your body, seven, eight, better and better, nine, and ten, all the way into your body and feeling great. Open the elevator door and be where you are.

9

INTERFERENCE and BLOCKS to EXPERIENCING the INNER SHAMAN

Our mythic story is a powerful method of understanding why so many people have trouble connecting with the Inner Shaman, why there is resistance to knowing this fabulous resource. Without such stories, we have difficulty understanding the scope of our grand experiment, the reason for our suffering, and the possibility of regaining our freedom. The creation myth of the mini-mes gives an insight into the nature of the obstacles, the reason why there is an opposing team that tries to defeat us on the path to our goal. Unlike the statistical explanations of science, our creation myth makes it clear that we are involved in a grand game, and like any game there are ways to win and ways to lose—but if we lose, we lose only temporarily, because we designed the game to end ultimately in victory.

When this real-appearing dream, what we consider to be reality, occurred as a result of our curiosity, the false personality or parasite was created along with it. The parasite arose because this "reality" was a physical universe based on the concept of separate units. Atoms, electrons, and so on appear to be separate from one another. (Yet as you have seen, quantum physics is now speculating that this is not really so—that everything is connected.) The job of the false personality is to dominate the physical plane, reinforce its tendencies toward fragmentation, and prevent its dissolution. It feeds on drama and anything that creates more separation, just as a forest fire feeds on trees and brush. We, the mini-mes, through our desire to experience a universe without Spirit, made the false personality. You could say that this experimental game was a big success. Shamans regard the false personality as a worthy opponent, not a simple pushover. The dissolution of the physical plane happens when people wake up from the dream of separation. Does that mean the physical universe just vanishes when we wake up? No. It does not disappear right away because it has inertia, momentum for a time.

According to shamanic lore, the physical universe is temporary and will vanish someday, disappearing into the void from which it came. In the meantime, it is possible to replace the dreamlike nightmares of the physical plane—war, poverty, illness, and hunger—with light and the brilliance of a beautiful new dream that resonates with Spirit. The dream can be much more wonderful than it has been thus far. First we will be greeted by cooperation, love, compassion, forgiveness, bliss, joy, and happiness. Then, when the physical plane is no longer needed as a platform for remembering, it will simply vanish, as night dreams vanish when we awaken to a new day. To get there, the false personality, the author of self-importance, must be dethroned one person at a time until there is no one left who believes it. This is the way the old false gods died off—through lack of attention. This may take some time, from a physical plane point of view. In eternity, it will take no time at all. In fact, shamans believe it already happened before the game even began; we are just finding out. That is why shamans are not fearful. They have seen the outcome of the game. They know the truth.

THE FALSE PERSONALITY: A WORTHY OPPONENT

Shamans are under no illusion that people are without flaws and defects. They understand better than anyone that humans have a shadow side, because much of their training is devoted to cleaning out the darkness that obscures the bright light. They know what a long, hard road this can be. They learn not to judge others for their flaws but simply to help people to heal from them. They know that the minute they judge and blame, they are doomed to be controlled by that which they condemn. So, for the most part, shamans are kind and compassionate with others but ruthless when it comes to facing off with the challenger. This is where the warrior in every shaman shows up.

Lest you think I am exaggerating the wiliness of the false personality, realize that shamans understand that in the game of life there are strong challenges and great obstacles to overcome. After all, any game worth its salt has obstacles and challenges. If the game is too easy it is not considered fun. No one would go to see an NFL football team play against a high school team. But if the obstacles are too great, no one wants to play; there has to be a reasonable possibility of winning. At odds of zero percent, few people would gamble. The best games have two equally matched teams fighting it out for victory. Therefore, for the mini-mes, the opposing team in the game of life, the false personality, has to be tough. Stepping on an ant is not fighting a worthy opponent. Wrestling a bear is. This is what Don Juan, Carlos Castenedas teacher, referred to as a petty tyrant.

The false personality is a pretend consciousness that relies on the perception of separation in order to maintain its storyline. It lives off the vitality of Spirit by distorting its message and diverting it to its own aims and goals. This is why Toltec shamans call the false personality the parasite—because it masquerades as the real thing while living off its host and eventually killing it, just as the HIV virus does in the body. So successful is the false personality that most people do not have a clue how destructive it is to awareness. It is a world-class hypnotist and it will coopt anything and everything to maintain its dominance of the physical universe.

For centuries, the false personality has been able to convince people that the universe is an accident of nature conforming to real, fixed laws that cannot be transcended, even though the evidence is everywhere—according to quantum physicists as well as shamans—that this is simply not so. Although miraculous events happen every day, proving beyond doubt that these laws can be suspended, skeptics have managed to convince most of the scientific community that they are not valid. Physicians regularly ignore miracles of healing, while the media ignores one of the biggest anomalies of our time—crop circles. Scientists, especially historians and geologists, ignore the anomalies that do not fit into their theories. Religious organizations are dedicated to ignoring whatever does not fit their dogma.

The false personality convinces people of the existence of enemies, makes them believe that they must protect themselves against one another and must destroy the planet to save themselves from their greatest fears. Thus the false personality spreads its poisonous doctrine of paradox, pain, suffering, and death while trying to hide clues to the truth that all is one. No wonder so many people cannot find the Inner Shaman; the false personality is busy creating distractions. What a worthy opponent it is!

The false personality is the ego consciousness spoken of in Buddhism and alluded to as Satan by Christians, though it has never been a living entity, a devil. The favorite activity of the false personality is distraction. Everyone who has reared young children knows how successful distraction is when trying to get a child to stop crying or screaming. The favorite tool of the false personality for creating distraction is thought: endless thoughts explaining, comparing, judging, processing, analyzing, figuring, considering, denying, agreeing, arguing, blaming, identifying, and on and on. Humans have elevated thought to the golden throne and proclaimed it king. Yet thought can be a huge troublemaker when it is separated from its source, the higher mind that resides in the heart. When thought is divorced from the higher mind, it falls prey to fear.

The false personality uses fear as its major distraction and motivation for thought processes. It loves to lob fearful thought grenades into your mind so that you will react with more fear. Then it consumes the products of this fear and becomes stronger, and you become weaker. If you do not react, the grenade does not explode and then you get stronger, but if you take the bait and react, the grenade explodes and you suffer miserably, unable to sleep, worrying, crying, or struggling. Shamans the world over identify these fears as primarily twofold: fear of abandonment and fear of imprisonment. These two fears break down into the seven fear patterns I refer to in my articles and books as Obstacles or Dragons. In a nutshell, they are self-destruction, greed, self-deprecation, arrogance, martyrdom, impatience, and stubbornness. You can read about how to overcome these fear patterns in great detail in my book *Transforming Your Dragons*.

EXERCISE **HANDLING THE FALSE PERSONALITY IN ACTION**

In order to do this exercise most effectively, you will have to wait until the false personality is activated. Don't worry: you won't have to wait long. It rises up most typically in response to stress, such as being late for an appointment or being annoyed with someone. However, you can simply recall a recent event of this kind and that will allow you to do the exercise right now.

1. Recall a recent situation where you reacted angrily or defensively to someone, became very insecure and fearful, reacted by becoming impatient or stubborn, became overly needy, felt unworthy, became judgmental and critical, became whiny and complaining, or did something self-destructive. Can you feel this again in retrospect?

2. Recognize that the minute this reaction began to take place you were coopted by the false personality and it began to run you.

3. Now in your imagination, stop the action and look at what was happening within you. Try to pinpoint when and how it started. When did you start to feel bad? First John said this, then I thought that, then he responded, and then I felt criticized and hurt and got defensive and so on.

4. Notice that somewhere in this picture there was some fear. As best you can, identify the fear: was it fear of being abandoned, fear of being trapped, fear of losing time, fear of losing out, fear of being judged or not accepted, fear of being forced or controlled, fear of being victimized, or some other fear?

5. Recognize that there is no objective world out there and that this drama is and was happening entirely

in your own imagination even if it appeared quite real at the time.

6. Now, firmly and with conviction, say to your fear and the false personality it stems from: "I see you. I see what you are trying to do to distract me. I am not buying it this time. You have no power over me. Get lost."

7. You may have to do this several times, but in the end you will prevail. It is like developing a muscle; it will strengthen over time. Good work, uncomfortable but productive.

THE FILTERS OF DISTORTION

Let us take a moment to revisit the filters of imprinting mentioned earlier, in chapter 3. You now know that the Inner Shaman sits quiet and protected in the heart—not in the middle of your head. The job of the Inner Shaman is to speak through the heart—the other brain—not through your thinking head, known as the cerebrum. Knowing this, the false personality has arranged a series of blocking filters between the Inner Shaman and your heart. This cuts off much of the life force from entering your system and limits the truth, love, and energy entering your heart.

The false personality inserts additional filters between your sense organs and your brain, containing imprinted beliefs and conditioning instead of the truth of your heart. When you see the world through your eyes, and hear the world through your ears, you perceive dangers, threats, and limitations that cause you to act from the prejudices of your culture, your religion, and your family of origin. You may be afraid of people of different skin color, alternative sexual preference, or religious belief. Your fear causes you to want to attack them, get rid of them, banish them. Your socially imprinted beliefs cause you to feel small, guilty, ashamed, unable to find Spirit, unable to find love, unable to accomplish your vision. You begin to act from defensiveness, revenge, judgment, bitterness, greed, envy, prejudice, gossip, slander, and a host of other behaviors that, instead of producing happiness, produce anxiety, hostility, and depression.

As long as there are filters of distortion interrupting the flow of influence from the Inner Shaman, you will suffer, because the power of the Inner Shaman is being blocked from doing its supreme job: connecting you with Spirit. Bear in mind that the Inner Shaman is still doing its job, because nothing can prevent it from doing that. Rather, you have accepted the filters and are not listening to the Inner Shaman. Nor are you a victim of this state of affairs. In a deeper sense we are all the authors of the distorting filters, the imprinting, the conditioning, the false beliefs, the societies and families that program us, the false personality itself.

EXERCISE **CLEARING THE DISTORTING FILTERS**

1. Sit in a relaxed and comfortable position, and make sure there are no distractions or interruptions. This may mean silencing the cell phone and benevolently banishing the dog or cat from the room.

2. Memorize the following sequence: Refresh, renew, restore, recalibrate, raise the frequency of, and clean the filters from . . .

3. Now you are ready to go. Repeat: "Refresh, renew, restore, recalibrate, raise the frequency of, and clean

the filters from the ocular nerve. Remove all filters
that prevent my seeing what I am meant to see."

4. Hearing: Repeat the sequence, ending with: ". . .
   and clean the filters from the nerves of the inner ear.
   Remove all filters that prevent my hearing what I
   am meant to hear."

5. Sensing: Repeat the sequence, ending with: ". . .
   clean all filters from my pituitary gland and pineal
   gland. Remove all filters that prevent me from
   sensing what I am meant to sense at this time."

6. Repeat this sequence a couple of times a week,
   as the filters need cleaning often. The whole
   sequence should take no longer than about two
   or three minutes.

10

ENTHRONING the INNER SHAMAN

There are at least eight things that the false personality hates and regards as enemies. The first is meditation, because that is what the Inner Shaman loves to do—and it is thus a very effective way to enthrone your Inner Shaman. Meditation is the practice of quieting the thoughts of the mind, so that the voice of essence or the Inner Shaman may be heard and the voice of the false personality is silenced. There are countless forms of meditation, which come from a great many traditions. You can learn special meditation techniques or you can simply practice keeping your mind empty. Despite its simplicity, meditation is a discipline and it may take you a while to become good at it.

Many people confuse concentration with meditation. There is a difference. Concentration is the practice of focusing on something to occupy your thoughts. Meditation is the practice of having no thoughts at all. Both are very helpful, but here we are talking about meditation. To prepare for meditation, I find it good to do some chi gong or yoga to open the body and its energy channels.

Even though there are numerous forms of meditation, formal practice is not required. I prefer simple forms of meditation such as the ones below. You can mix and match as you please as long as you do something, anything, every day.

If you do any of these meditation exercises on a regular basis, with a bit of discipline, you will be successful at quieting your mind. Remember that meditation is not supposed to be torturous or a huge effort. It should feel good. If you are struggling and suffering, stop and try again when you are in a different state. It is also a good idea to do a short practice of meditation at the same time every day. I like to do it first thing in the morning.

EXERCISE **BREATHING AND LETTING GO**

1. Reside in that space two inches behind the bridge of the nose. Perform yogic breathing: Breathing in, the abdomen goes out. Breathing out, the abdomen pulls in and up.

2. Ride the infinite tiny moments of now and accept the inevitability of what is.

3. Breathing in, say to yourself: "Accepting." Let everything be as it is right now in your life. Breathing out say to yourself: "Releasing." See, sense, or feel as various things go rushing out through the top of your head. You do not have to know what they are. You will feel better, lighter, and more focused.

EXERCISE **LETTING THOUGHTS GO**

1. Sit in a relaxed position with no distractions.

2. Watch each thought as it arises into your awareness.

3. Notice that while it appears to be your thought, it is simply a thought, not yours, not anyone's. Do not identify with it or allow it to produce more similar thoughts.

4. Let it go past.

5. Await the next thought that arises. Continue to follow the same process.

6. Gradually your thoughts will come more slowly. That is good. You are making progress.

CONTEMPLATION

The second enemy of the false personality is contemplation. Contemplation is not ordinary thinking; rather, it is penetrating insight, powerful and deep awareness, seeing the truth behind the lie. Rather than using the comparing and judging qualities of the left brain, contemplation uses the holistic properties of the right brain. Contemplation is threatening to the false personality because it wrests away control and takes charge of what thoughts you are having.

You can invite the spirit of contemplation in many different ways: play music, use aromatherapy, or place a bouquet of fresh-cut fragrant flowers in front of you. By focusing your senses, you are keeping them busy. Your sensations are happening in the moment of now and they keep you present, the better to focus on your contemplation.

Ideally, contemplation is best done outdoors in a beautiful natural setting such as a beach, mountain, meadow, or desert environment. You can enhance your contemplation by holding certain rocks, crystals, or semiprecious stones in your hands or by placing them strategically at the top of the head. They are allies and can help you to focus, raise your inspiration level, or help to open your heart. Some of my favorites are Tibetan black quartz crystal, apophylite, sugilite, calcite, lapis lazuli, azurite, lingam stone, and chrysacola.

EXERCISE **CONTEMPLATING GREAT QUESTIONS**

1. You may begin with an open topic in mind, such as the nature of time, the influence of the heart, or the illusion of the senses. These may begin as simple musings or questions. You might ask, "How is it that time is rushing by but I am still always right here?" Perhaps you might ask, "Who am I?" or "Who am I when I am not wearing my body?"

2. Stay in your heart. Then allow the Inner Shaman to teach you, to answer your questions. Be sure to listen. At first you may not hear anything, but with practice you will find that you are given clear responses.

I often keep a notepad next to me to jot down a word or phrase I can come back to later. However, it is better not to engage in extensive note-taking, or you will defeat the purpose of contemplation. Until you have more experience, avoid anxiety-provoking topics such as "What should I do with my life?" or "How should I handle this difficult relationship with X?"

The purpose of contemplation is to examine an idea and through your close examination become transformed by what you learn. Contemplation should lead to something that is a game-changer for you, an insight that makes you see the world in an entirely different way. Contemplation should shake your world, get you to question a belief system, or show you clearly that there is another way to perceive the world. The contemplations below are designed to do just that. But do not restrict yourself to these few examples. Take something that you would like to question and contemplate it.

EXERCISE **VARIOUS POWERFUL**
QUESTIONS TO CONTEMPLATE

1. Contemplate the fact that in people with multiple personalities, the subpersonalities can have completely different medical conditions. One subpersonality, when it is front and center, may show all the symptoms of diabetes and need to take insulin, yet when another subpersonality shows up, the body has no symptoms at all and taking insulin will kill it. As each subpersonality appears, the body instantly produces all the symptoms that that subpersonality believes it has. How can this be? What does it suggest about the body, about who people think they are, and belief systems in general?

2. Contemplate the fact that an idiot savant may know everything about a certain topic without ever having studied it or been exposed to it. How can this be? How does this person have access to this information, especially when they have a damaged brain? Where is information like this stored? In the brain? In the quantum field? In the DNA? What are the implications for everyone? Could you gain access to this information too? Why not?

3. Contemplate the fact that gravity works on everything but not on thoughts. If thoughts are not held down by gravity, can they travel? Do all your thoughts originate with you? If not, where do they come from? Does God have thoughts? Can you have the same thoughts as God has?

4. Contemplate the fact that under hypnosis, a person may be able to speak a foreign language which they have never studied, and have no recollection afterward.

5. Contemplate the fact that under the influence of certain plant medicines, a person with no knowledge of music may play the piano like a virtuoso, and a person who has never been able to carry a tune can sing in a beautiful voice.

6. If only 3 percent of your DNA is protein-based, what is the rest of your DNA made of? If some plants and animals have more gene sequences than humans, what makes humans smarter or more complex? Does DNA all know the same thing since it is identical in makeup? What does DNA know, and is there anything it does not know?

CONCENTRATION

A third tool of the Inner Shaman and enemy of the false personality is concentration. Concentration differs from contemplation in that it is a specific focus, using visualization or another method, where all attention is placed on a subject or object. For example, you may wish to concentrate on your chakras by visualizing different colors of light for each one, or concentrate on what you are hearing, seeing, sensing, feeling, etc.

EXERCISE **THE GLOWING MUSTARD SEED**

1. Start by focusing on a tiny mustard seed in the navel area, or *tan tien* as it is known in chi gong, three-quarters of an inch below your navel and several inches inside.

2. See an electric blue light growing from the seed there, a ball of light. Focus on this for a few minutes or up to an hour. You will see, sense, or feel the light beginning to penetrate throughout your body, especially to those places that have problems, healing them.

3. Next, raise the mustard seed to your heart and see, sense, or feel the light emanating from it, growing and radiating all through your chest and upper back. The light will have a crystalline, sunlike quality, and may become very bright and be accompanied by a strong sensation.

4. After a time, raise the mustard seed to your throat, specifically the thyroid area, and have it grow into a beautiful crystalline light. Make it as intense as possible.

5. After a time, raise the mustard seed to the brow and repeat the process of concentration.

6. After a time, raise the mustard seed to the crown of your head and repeat the process. This would be a very good time to pray or make decrees.

Many shamans believe that your spirit enters your body just below your skull, at the place where your spinal column enters your head: the brain stem. Therefore, that spot is considered by many to be the seat of consciousness. Focusing your attention there can have powerful results.

If you reach behind your neck and follow your spinal cord up until it enters the bony cranium, you will be at the brain stem and medulla area. The medulla oblongata is a longer, snakelike organ just below the medulla that is sometimes referred to by spiritual teachers as the mouth of God.

1. Focus on your brain stem and visualize a golden ball of light, like a miniature sun, in the area of the medulla.

2. Reinforce the golden sun's light with each breath. Eventually, let three streams of golden light flow out of the golden ball through your eyes and your forehead just above the bridge of your nose. Several feet in front of you, a triangle will form and, if you are a good visualizer, a golden Madonna or goddess figure may appear, looking at you with the most loving, kind, and compassionate expression. Observe and enjoy the sensation of being nurtured like this by the feminine face of Spirit.

3. A variation calls for 10 percent of the golden light to bounce back to the brain stem from your three eyes. The light bounces forward and back quickly, like a ping-pong ball, for as long as you do the exercise. This bathes the pineal and pituitary gland in a golden light, activating, refreshing, and cleaning them.

EXERCISE **AUM**

This exercise is a concentration on a sound that you can make yourself. Some would say it is a form of chanting. Hindus, as well as Tibetan Buddhists, believe that an underlying sound is the vibration of the universe. The Hindus say it is AUM and the Tibetans say it is OM. When you repeat these sounds, you put yourself into harmony with the cosmos.

1. Breathe in and on the exhale tone: "AAAAAAAHHHHH." Then, before running out of breath: "UUUUUUUUU." Then, before running out of breath: "MMMMMMMMM." Try to give them equal time and keep it brief, so you don't run out of breath before you finish.

2. Pay attention to each sound and follow the vibration where you feel it rising up your body, starting at the heart, moving to the throat, and finally the brow.

3. Repeat as long as you wish. This is extremely powerful, because you are working with sound vibration, so do it often. Every day would be a good frequency.

ACCEPTANCE

A fourth enemy of the false personality and friend of the Inner Shaman is nonresistance or acceptance, cultivating the practice of becoming neutral about all external appearances. Numerous Buddhist stories illustrate this notion. In one, a young novice and a monk are traveling together along the road and as they go they talk. The novice wants to know why Buddhist teachings recommend nonattachment to outcome. To illustrate, the monk tells the novice a story about a boy living in a village with his father.

More than anything in the world, the boy wanted a horse. He begged his father to buy him one—and after a time he relented and got him a spirited horse. All the townspeople said how great this was. One day, the horse was startled by a snake and threw the boy, causing him to break his leg. Everyone said how terrible it was that he had gotten the horse. But then there was a draft for a new war being waged and because the boy had broken his leg, the military would not take him. Everyone said how good it was that he had broken his leg, that it saved his life.

The story went on and on, with each event sending the people back and forth between judgments of great and terrible. Yet their judgments could never foresee what was to happen next so they were always wrong in their assessment. The only correct assessment was no assessment at all—or, in other words, simple acceptance of events.

In a second story, a Buddhist monk lived in a village where he was highly respected by the townspeople. They told him how wonderful it was that he lived among them. To their comments he replied, "Oh, is that so?" One day a teenage girl became pregnant and, when her parents asked her who the father was, she accused the monk of raping her. The townspeople were very angry and threatened him, saying he was a very bad man. They told him they would put him in jail. To all this the monk said, "Oh, is that so?" A few days later, the girl confessed that she had accused him falsely and revealed that the real father was a teenage boy who lived across the village. All the townspeople once again said what a good man the monk was, and to all this the monk said, "Oh, is that so?" The story goes on and on, with various events leading the people to alternately condemn and exonerate the monk. Refusing to be swept up in their fantasies, he maintained the neutral position, holding no opinion of what he knew was pure folly or maya.

In both of these tales you can see that acceptance of what is, offering no resistance to what you don't agree with or what you don't want, prevents the monk from losing his way in drama and worry. When you are all-accepting, the false personality has nothing to work with; you slowly starve it of extreme emotional content, which is its food. The Inner Shaman eventually shines through more brightly and clearly.

EXERCISE **STAYING NEUTRAL**

1. Think of an event where you became angry at what people said about you. Consider all the painful feelings this situation caused you.

2. Now, see if you can accept what happened without being attached to one outcome or another. If you wish, you can borrow the Buddhist monk's phrase, "Oh, is that so," as you consider each of your leftover feelings.

3. Accept the other players in this drama as simply characters reciting their lines in order to provide you with a test. How did you do on this test? Did you lose your neutrality? Can you chuckle about it now? What part still sticks in your mind?

4. Keep don't-know mind.

Nonjudgment

The fifth enemy of the false personality is nonjudgment—what the Buddhists refer to as compassion, or what Christians term forgiveness. Shamanically speaking, this powerful ally of the Inner Shaman is called "seeing." All of these words refer to a particular form of nonresistance whereby one takes responsibility for one's experience by not blaming or judging anyone for anything. In this form of practice, you "see" all people and events as projections of your own psyche, distortions of the truth, the truth being that they are all aspects of yourself. When you forgive them, you take all the energy out of your projections, and this releases you from being trapped by the tangles of judgment and bitterness between you. You are free.

Ho'oponopono

The indigenous Hawaiian practice of Ho'oponopono is excellent for practicing the art of nonjudgment. Hawaii consists of islands, so when there was conflict between tribes there was no place to escape and it would quickly escalate into carnage. The local kahunas, the Hawaiian shamans, devised Ho'oponopono as a method to avoid this terrible warfare and pave the way for peaceful coexistence. The practice turned out to be terrifically successful.

There are twelve steps in a complete Ho'oponopono ceremony. The four primary steps of simple applied Ho'oponopono are:

1. Apologizing for whatever the unfortunate experience was—no matter who appeared to cause it, even if there seems to be a clear victim: "I am sorry that this happened, that we are both distraught and unhappy."

2. Forgiving all involved, including oneself. No blame. "I forgive you and I forgive me."

3. Saying, "I love you" to all involved, including oneself.

4. Thanking all, including oneself, for the lessons provided and lessons learned. "Thank you for teaching me."

EXERCISE **HO'OPONOPONO**

1. Think of a conflict you have had with someone, or one that you are currently experiencing. It can involve more than one person—a group or an organization. Recall all the parties and what is involved. You can even choose a conflict on the world stage that you are not personally connected with.

2. Now, get the sense that you are apologizing on a higher level for all the pain and suffering that this situation has resulted in. This is not about assigning blame or fault. It is a sincere apology that there has been unpleasantness, bad blood, anger, grief, and pain on all sides. "I am truly sorry you have suffered and for anything I may have done to contribute to this problem." You are speaking from the larger "I Am," not from your personality with its petty opinions.

3. Now, take the position of Spirit and forgive all the players. "I forgive you for X. I forgive me for Y." This is like a reset, starting the game over.

4. Again taking the benevolent and loving position of Spirit, say simply, "I love you. You and I are one being." Remember that you are included in the love.

5. Now, viewing the whole situation afresh, see the lessons learned and say, "Thank you for being instrumental in teaching me what I needed to learn." Here you are thanking the actors for an excellent performance for your benefit.

This exercise is most effective when you can come from the heart and mean what you say. To do so, you must step away from blame and attachment to your story. This exercise is incomprehensibly powerful when done well.

Erasing Fear

The sixth tool of the Inner Shaman and enemy of the false personality is erasing all forms of fear, the ego's favorite emotions to feed on. Here are some simple qualities of fear that are important not to forget:

- Fear occupies the same space that love normally occupies. Where fear is, love cannot be and vice versa.

- Love always conquers fear in the end because it is more powerful.

- Fear begets more of itself. In other words, fear always makes you more fearful if you indulge in it. The worst forms of fear end in catastrophes, such as world wars and genocide.

- Fear generates personality defenses that in the end always produce what you are most afraid of. Thus, if you are afraid of losing time you will rush about, causing an accident that makes you lose even more time.

- Fear is usually about something that is not real. It is based on what might happen. Therefore, most fears are hallucinations.

One simple way to meet your fear head on is to form the habit of saying, "Fear is never justified," every time something causes you anxiety, fear, or worry. You can practice this after bad dreams, after the startle reaction that Spanish-speaking shamans call a *susto*, such as when you have a near miss in traffic or when walking in a dangerous neighborhood at night.

I was once traveling in Bolivia on a reconnaissance trip for one of my shamanic training groups when a strike brought all the buses and taxis to a halt. I had to walk several miles, dragging my wheeled bag behind me, to the border. On the road I encountered a big dog that approached me, snarling. I had a visceral fear response, but, understanding the nature of dogs, I forced myself to look at the dog neutrally and began to repeat out loud, "Fear is never justified." I focused on the meaning of this phrase—that I was creating the problem through my fear and that there was nothing actually to fear. The minute I started to do this, the dog stopped and turned away. I walked on, marveling at the power of this method. In this situation, the dog was my teacher.

In most situations, there is nothing to fear, and our fear reaction is the thing that gets us into deeper trouble. That is why the shamanic path teaches the neutralizing of fear. The less fear we have, the more power we can access.

SERVICE

The seventh tool of the Inner Shaman to defeat the false personality is the act of service, known as right work by Buddhists and karma yoga by Hindus. By making a positive contribution to furthering awareness and love, no matter how small or how modest, we cut through the manipulations of the false personality. Service cuts through our self-importance and keeps us focused on giving rather than getting.

All human beings have a life task, a mission, to accomplish, with specific lessons to learn, agreements to keep, and karma to erase. This is vastly easier to accomplish when we are willing to give of ourselves unselfishly to ameliorate the delusion of separation, to support and help ourselves and others to wake up in whatever way is appropriate, while at the same time allowing each person the freedom to pursue whatever beliefs they choose.

The tradition of service in shamanism is legendary. Shamans throughout time have been known for their extraordinary ability to conduct healing sessions and ceremonies that last many days and nights. They work extremely hard, usually for modest pay, providing good counsel for the people of their tribe, predicting weather and hunting conditions, and gathering herbs and plants, sometimes by the light of the full moon, to heal their patients. When they are not being of service, they are busy preparing themselves, learning, gathering knowledge and power, and disciplining themselves to become even better at what they do.

Acts of service may be accomplished by volunteering at a soup kitchen, a homeless shelter, or even an animal shelter. However, most people don't realize that acts of service can be performed anywhere at any time, without actually volunteering any direct action. Here is one of my favorites:

EXERCISE **GIVING GIFTS SILENTLY**

1. Go to a public place such as an airport, a bus terminal, or even a park bench on a busy walkway, and station yourself strategically so you can watch people without being intrusive.

2. Select various individuals at random and choose to give them a gift. You do not engage them physically in any way. Here comes a man with a cane: you give him good health and better mobility. Maybe you take his pain away. Here comes a downcast person: you give her happiness, perhaps greater connection with Spirit. Here comes a child: you give her a bright future. Here comes someone who looks poor: you give him greater prosperity and more resources.

Here comes someone who looks angry: you give him love and forgiveness. And so on.

3. You will probably never see any of these people again, so you will have no way of knowing whether your gifts were received or not. That is good. You do not need confirmation.

FASTING

The eighth tool of the Inner Shaman is fasting. This is not rocket science: when you go without eating, the body has a chance to detoxify, which renders it a more sensitive instrument for Spirit. When you go without eating, your body has a chance to rest from all the energy going into digestion, making this energy available for higher-centered activity.

When fasting, it is best to start with a single day in which you drink only juice or a blend of water, maple syrup, and cayenne. This is sometimes called "the master cleanse." After your body has adapted with this brief fast, work toward going to three days. Do this once a month. Next, you can try a five-day fast, working up to a ten-day fast. During the longer fasts you should refrain from hard labor or doing anything that takes great attention, such as driving a car. There are many specialized fasts, especially among indigenous peoples, who are experts regarding fasting with special plants. This is a very complex topic on which I encourage you to get guidance, but it is well worth it if you are serious about making steady progress toward erasing the false personality. Fasting combined with meditation and contemplation is a powerhouse tool of the Inner Shaman.

All the tools of the Inner Shaman discussed in this chapter are tried and true, practiced by millions of people around the world over many thousands of years. They have often been adopted by mainstream religions as part of their practices. Many religions advocate meditation, contemplation, service, fasting, and the like, but they were not the first to designate these practices as powerful methods of advancement. All of them borrowed these practices from other traditions that came before them. Christians and Buddhists sometimes forget that their founders were realized masters who were exposed to the teachings of earlier traditions. Jesus borrowed heavily from Zoroaster, Krishna, and the Egyptian practitioners, who in turn got their powerful methods from even earlier traditions, the shamanic traditions that came earliest of all.

Over the millennia, many teachers have added tidbits to this or that practice, sometimes enhancing them and sometimes burdening them with complexity or making them too extreme. When in doubt, it is always a good idea to go back to the basics and not to overdo any one practice. The best practice involves using all these methods in balance. You do not have to meditate twenty hours a day to make good progress. Remember that as with all things, quality is better than quantity.

11

CULTIVATING the INNER SHAMAN

When we acknowledge the inner shaman and live from Source, we can do pretty much anything of which we can conceive. The reason for this is simple: since what we experience as reality is actually a dream, a realistic hallucination, everything we see, feel, and experience is a symbolic dream projection. This projection includes how we experience other people. When we perceive another person, we are looking at a distortion. All people that we see have an Inner Shaman within their hearts. But that Inner Shaman is actually our own Inner Shaman projected onto what seems like a person over there. Therefore, there are not multiple Inner Shamans—only one grand Inner Shaman being experienced in what seems like a variety of places. Your Inner Shaman is my Inner Shaman and mine is yours. When I acknowledge my Inner Shaman, I am actually acknowledging all the forms of the Inner Shaman everywhere and in doing so I am waking them all up, if ever so slightly. When I meet you and see the Inner Shaman in you, it stirs and becomes brighter, more radiant, with more light. As that happens, so does the Inner Shaman in me become brighter and more radiant, because they are all in communication. By definition, they are all one, as an aspen forest is one root system with multiple trees springing out of it.

One day several years ago, I was boarding a flight from Chicago back to New Mexico after a few days' work, tired but feeling extremely good about what had transpired on the trip. I had upgraded my seat, so I entered the plane ahead of the crowd and sat in business class. Normally I would have pulled out a book and dived into it, but this time I felt the urge to watch the other passengers as they entered the plane and walked past me. Usually I am entertained by the odd cast of characters, the people of different soul ages, and the variety of men and women, children, and older folks entering a plane. This time, as they started to file by, I noticed a bright, crystalline glow emanating from each person's chest. I immediately became aware that this was the Inner Shaman, what Christians call the Christ force and what Buddhists call Buddha nature, the great equalizer, that which made each person exactly the same as me. Fascinated, I watched person after person walk by. This time there was no judgment, no evaluation of soul age, and no notice taken of whether they were male or female, fat or thin, young or old. They were all "I Am." Even when I tried to interest myself in the fact that one was a beautiful woman, I found I couldn't do it. She was the same as everyone else.

As I watched them all go by, I felt higher and higher and my chest was fairly bursting with its own light as the last one went by. I simply marveled at the power of the experience.

THE POWER OF OPERATING FROM THE BIG PICTURE

When you learn to operate from the stance of the big picture, as described in the story above, you become extraordinarily powerful because you are working with every Inner Shaman everywhere. When you operate from your ordinary personality, without the knowledge of the Inner Shaman, you have the power of only a fragment of your total self. Most people live as if they are fragments, and thus their power is severely curtailed. The choice is between having the power of one person or having the power of the human species and all sentient beings at your fingertips. This seems obvious, but the ego is so clever, so wily, that it makes sure almost everyone chooses to operate from the limited power of their imagined isolated self. If this did not feel so bad it would be utterly laughable, totally absurd, unimaginable.

So how do you go about cultivating your Inner Shaman? How do you invite it to emerge from the shadows? Shamanically speaking, where your attention goes, so goes your power. If your attention begins to go to the Inner Shaman for a part of each day, your power goes there and activates this powerhouse within. All master shamans have fully activated their Inner Shaman, without exception. This is what allows them to do the many extraordinary things they do, such as traveling to other star systems, healing with the power of touch, vanishing into thin air, and leaping over mountains. Knowing they are dreaming their reality, they can become lucid in their dream, which gives them power over the dream. The alternative is to be a victim of the dream—an absurdity to shamans since they know they are the dreamers.

A couple of years ago, I had the good fortune to visit Q'eros, an extremely rugged high-altitude region in the Andes of Peru. There I met Modesto, an Andean paqo to whose daughter I became godfather. Modesto has a severe hip displacement problem that makes walking a very slow, painstaking affair. This was a result of being struck by lightning when he was five years old. Despite his physical disability, Modesto exhibits what all Andean paqos seem to display: a shining and sunny disposition coupled with exceptional modesty and friendliness. After spending some time with his family, we mounted our horses for an arduous day's ride over rough terrain in the 15,000-foot range to another village. After many hours, we arrived and began to set up camp. A few minutes later, Modesto appeared, smiling brightly and walking his very slow walk over to greet us. There was no way he could have walked fast enough to keep up with the horses and riding was not an option for him. He simply showed up without obvious transport because in that part of the Andes there are no vehicles or roads, only horse and llama trails. How did he do it? He is a master of dreaming, a master of navigation in the dream, and distance and time are not obstacles for him. After all, he was struck by lightning, the sign of a powerful shaman in the Andes.

EXERCISE **OPENING A SHAMANIC PORTAL**

There are a variety of ways to access the Inner Shaman, some of which we have already discussed. In addition, there are various ways of opening shamanic portals or inner pathways leading to the Inner Shaman and to other dimensions. This is a powerful and effective one.

First, read over this exercise. Then close your eyes and do the process. For this exercise you will need to work with a vesica pisces. This is a fish shape formed when two circles of equal size, sitting next to each other, overlap each other to the center of the other circle. It is the shape of every orifice of your body— your mouth, nostrils, eyes, and so on. They are all entrances or portals into the body. This is considered a very sacred shape, acknowledged by shamans as a portal of power.

1. Imagine drawing two circles around your breasts so that the outside of each circle runs through the nipple on the opposite breast. Where they overlap, you will have a vesica pisces in the center of your chest. Feel the golden light emanating from it like a beacon in your chest. Allow the circles to enlarge, making the vesica pisces grow in size to encompass your whole body. Now your body is shining with golden light.

2. Focus on the Inner Shaman within your heart.

3. Notice in detail how the Inner Shaman appears today.

4. Feel the sensation in your heart as the Inner Shaman radiates with light and power.

5. Now, with an act of your will, realizing that your willingness is extremely powerful, allow the Inner Shaman to begin to grow ever so slowly.

6. Let the Inner Shaman grow larger, so that it leaves the chair or throne behind.

7. Feel the Inner Shaman as it begins to fill up your chest, moves down your legs and out your arms, and eventually, in a few minutes, grows to fill the outline of your body. The Inner Shaman has become as large as you—and you are now the Inner Shaman.

8. Open your eyes and look around you as the Inner Shaman. What is different? How do you feel? Enjoy and indulge in the experience.

9. Close your eyes again and imagine that you are able to watch yourself from one of the upper corners of your room or, if you are outside, imagine yourself on a tree branch or somewhere above where you can look back down on your form. Take a good look at what you and your Inner Shaman look like. Is there light? Has your appearance changed in any way? Are you dressed like yourself or like the Shaman you saw earlier? What do your eyes look like from this objective perspective? What is your presence like?

10. When you have finished exploring and examining the Inner Shaman, make sure you bring yourself back into your own skin. Always wiggle your toes and your fingers to make sure you are firmly back and ensconced within your body.

11. A variation of this is to continue to let the Inner Shaman grow until it is all around you and you are inside of its heart. Experience this. Then let it begin to shrink back to your size.

12. Now return the Inner Shaman to its inner throne or seat by willing that it shrink down to its tiny size inside your heart. Make the vesica pisces smaller until it is located in your chest.

Some people ask if it wouldn't be better to leave the Inner Shaman at its larger size—and this is a good question. Shamanism is a tidy tradition. All tools that are taken out for use are put away reverently and neatly until they are needed again. In the case of the Inner Shaman, though it may always be in use, it should be carefully returned to its place of greatest effectiveness for now.

Most of us are not prepared to handle the power of the Inner Shaman in its fully expressed state permanently. That comes with years of practice or with extraordinary maturity.

Leaving the Inner Shaman at full size may draw unwanted attention from others and may make you vulnerable to their curiosity and interest, something that at this stage you may find troublesome. Another danger is that your false personality can interfere and coopt the powers of the Inner Shaman for its own thought processes. Later, with practice and understanding, you will be able to handle all these things with aplomb. At this stage it is best to reduce self-importance, be humble and avoid arrogance or a desire for attention. The Inner Shaman will not lose any power by being small. It will only be easier for you to handle. Growing and shrinking the Inner Shaman is also good practice, as it exercises your ability to shift and move the most powerful of energies.

12

ENGAGING the INNER SHAMAN

lthough the Inner Shaman knows its job perfectly well, it does not intrude or interfere with the choices that your personality is making. It smiles, knowing that it is fully connected to Spirit at all times and that nothing can disturb it, nothing can harm it, nothing can distract it. When the personality finally gets around to acknowledging its presence, like the proverbial genie in the bottle, it responds by energetically saying, "Hello, welcome home. How can I assist you?" This gives you permission to give the Inner Shaman some instructions. This is a powerful moment and you should take advantage of it whenever it happens. Here is a suggested script, as an example of what you can say. Feel free to alter it with your own words and intentions; just make it respectful and absolutely clear. Remember that you are giving the Inner Shaman permission to step in and maximally help you.

"Inner Shaman, I want you to make it impossible to ignore you. I want you to give me unmistakable signs that you are helping me. I want every one of my experiences to be a healing experience. I want everything I say, everything I do, and everything I think to carry me one step closer to alignment with Spirit. I am on track now and I want you to help me remember to stay on track. You have my permission to remind me as often as necessary that you are there and to show me how to use you to best advantage. Do not allow me to remain distracted in the same old thought patterns, the same old habits that keep me asleep. Give me courage, focus, and help me clarify my highest vision for this life. Transform all my actions to prayers and all my thoughts to blessings. Help me set my priorities right. May every day bring more light, more clarity, more love, more truth, more power. Make it so. Aho, Amen."

Instruct the Inner Shaman to filter your thoughts so that all thoughts are in alignment with Spirit. In other words, when you are thinking, form the habit of thinking through your heart. This may sound strange, because we usually associate thinking with our heads. Just try thinking through your heart and see what happens. For example, you might be thinking about putting together materials for a building project or putting together an outline for a class or presentation. After instructing the Inner Shaman to help you think, tackle your agenda with regular attention—and focus on your heart, as often as you can. You are likely to find this process to be whole-hearted and productive.

ALIGNING THE INNER SHAMAN WITH YOUR HELPING SPIRITS

After you have learned to grow and reduce the Inner Shaman in size, you are in a position to work with it in a more advanced way. Here I am going to introduce you to the shamanic idea of helping spirits and totems. If you are already familiar with them, you can skip this brief section and move on to the exercise. Since we do not have space here for a treatise on the helping spirits, I am not going to explain them in any depth. It is sufficient that you know of them and address them in a very rudimentary way. The exercise below is a way to start becoming more connected with them.

We all have invisible guides that help us throughout life. Many of the major religions have put their own stamp on these guides, calling them angels and saints and so on that can be aligned with or petitioned for help. All traditions agree that there are sources of unseen support that people can call upon to help them in their challenges and tests. Sometimes they are represented in statues or figurines, to make the experience more real for the average person. Here I refer to them in the respectful shamanic way, as totems, power animals, teacher plants, nature spirits, grandfathers and grandmothers, sometimes ancestors, or master shamans who have passed on to the spirit world.

Helping spirits come to you. You do not decide which one you want and assume it is going to work with you. Many people think having a big animal or a giant mountain is impressive or more powerful than a kangaroo rat or a plant that grows close to the ground. This is not necessarily so.

I learned this the hard way. Once I was in a beautiful location in Alberta, Canada, where there were a great many eagles. I was about to conduct a healing ceremony with a group of people who would be arriving shortly. I looked around and assumed the eagles were there to support the ceremony and perhaps work with me, but I was wrong. I hunted around but found no eagle feathers left as gifts. I lay on the ground on my back as I had been taught and did a little journey, a visualization with eyes closed, and addressed the eagles. I asked them if they would work with me. Without any hesitation the eagles told me I was not ready to work with them and they were here for another purpose. They said that perhaps in a few years, if I worked hard, they might work with me. I was completely humbled.

Many years later, I was gifted with an eagle feather and given permission to use it as one of my healing tools. I worked with eagle in this way for many years. One day I was in California, starting a cross-country driving trip to a Lakota sun dance in South Dakota. I stopped at a roadside rest in the Sierras and offered some tobacco to my helping spirits for the success of the trip. I got an inner sense to look up and there, over my head, were two golden eagles winging their way eastward. I instantly knew the trip would be an outstanding success and I felt safe knowing they were guiding me. When I got to the sun dance, there were eagle feathers everywhere. That is the way it works.

Here is a brief exercise to help you become acquainted with your helping spirits. This exercise is often accompanied by a drum or rattle. If you do not have one with you, do not be concerned. You can still be successful doing this exercise. Coming to know your helping spirits can take many years. Shamans never finish the task because the helping spirits may change over time, so one must continue to connect with them.

EXERCISE **CONNECTING WITH YOUR HELPING SPIRITS**

1. Lie on your back, on the floor or preferably on the ground outside, and get as comfortable as possible, closing your eyes.

2. Visualize, sense, or feel that you are standing in front of an elevator, as we have done in earlier

exercises. Enter the elevator and go down slowly. Visualize or feel the floors dropping from ten to one.

3. Open the door and sense yourself in a beautiful outdoor environment. Ahead of you is a trail leading upward to a cliff face where there is an entrance to a cave or mine. Follow the trail and enter the opening. It is dark and goes way back. Ask for a guide to accompany you in the form of a colored light.

4. Ask the guide to lead you to meet one of your main helping spirits or several of them. Let it take you deep within the earth along various passageways. You may be traveling very quickly and you may wind around a number of tunnels going upward or downward. Do not be afraid.

5. Eventually the colored light will bring you to a destination. There may be someone there or the presence of an animal, plant, mountain, or element such as a raincloud or a fire. Observe, listen, feel, sense, or see whatever is present. Is there a message for you here? Does something say hello to you, speak to you, inform you in some way? If something appears threatening, move away from it. If something is friendly, move toward it.

6. See what you see, feel what you feel, hear what you hear. There is no right way to do this. This is just a tool to help you connect in some way with one or more of your guides.

7. Thank whatever guide(s) show up for their help. Ask them to continue to help you and to connect with you in more obvious ways.

8. Ask the colored light to take you back to where you started. Follow it back via the passages that you went through to get there.

9. Arrive back and enter the elevator. Go up from floor one to floor ten. Wiggle your toes and fingers. Open your eyes and take some notes if you wish.

Now you have the opportunity to ask your guides, totems, and power animals to align with the Inner Shaman, harmonize, and resonate at the same amplitude as it has. This is very important, as it reduces the chaos and chance of misalignment that can and does occur, making it hard at times to connect with your guides and helping spirits. The Inner Shaman is like the bass or drum setting the beat for the music. It is the core, connected to your source, and all other helpers are projections that are being asked to help you in your dreamscape. Yes, even power animals and guides are part of your dreamscape, projections of your own limitless self. If you don't recognize this, you can experience them as alien, as troublesome, as working out of harmony with you. This is a major distortion that shamans often get lost in. Don't allow it. You are the boss—not your delusional false personality, but you, aligned with the Inner Shaman.

This exercise supports you in coming into alignment and harmony with your helping spirits.

EXERCISE ALIGNING WITH YOUR HELPING SPIRITS

1. Get comfortable and take a series of deep breaths. Relax.

2. Follow the procedure to grow your Inner Shaman to full size. Visualize, sense, or feel your Inner Shaman growing from its small size in your heart to fill up your whole body.

3. Visualize yourself in an outdoor landscape of great beauty. Call upon your primary guides to appear before you or simply be present in symbolic form. For example, they may appear as a series of different colored lights. If you are already practiced in this type of journey work, then observe the various totems as they appear.

4. First, thank them for their tireless service on your behalf. Tell them you are now working with the Inner Shaman and you want them to align to that frequency from now on. If they are good for you, they will do this without hesitation. If not, it is time to bid them goodbye.

5. Draw a line connecting your heart to each of them.

6. Even if you are poor at visualizing, make this your intention and take whatever feedback is presented to you. In shamanism, you have to trust that what you are doing is effective, so again, even if you weren't able to see, sense, or feel anything, your intention covers it.

7. Return your Inner Shaman to its usual position in your heart.

Working with the Inner Shaman: Decreeing and Praying

After you have aligned all of your helping spirits with the Inner Shaman, you are now in a position to pray the most powerful prayers you have ever uttered. You may use various forms, but it is most important that you include all of the elements in the example below. At the beginning of this book I discussed the power of the word, the action component of Spirit that human beings all share, the ability to voice commands or decree creations. Here is a way you can voice sound as it was meant to be used.

Your prayer should be in the form of a decree, because you are praying with or from the Inner Shaman, not to the Inner Shaman. It is best to go outside to pray, but if weather or circumstances do not permit, being indoors is fine.

Start like this:

"Light above, light below, light within.
In the name of Truth, the Supreme Being [Great Spirit, God, Creator, Source]. In the name of love, the manifestation of Spirit that I Am, and in the name of the purest power of Spirit."

Spread out your arms and hands if you are comfortable with this.

"I bless this shaman who is in alignment with Spirit.
May he/she manifest in the fullest expression of Spirit at this time.
As this powerful shaman, may I be eternally grateful for my life and the freedom I have been given.
As this eternal shaman, may my mind be healed completely and with finality.
As this extraordinary shaman, may I be whole, perfect, supremely loved, and loving.

As this powerful shaman, may I forgive all
and be forgiven all.
Bless all beings asleep and awake,
May their dreams be of great beauty, love,
and potency.
Bless the Sky and Earth that they may be filled
with light and power.
Bless all the plants, the animals, and the elements
that they may serve Spirit and be completely fulfilled
in their mission.
May I be in harmony and resonance with them all.
Bless all aspects of the Great Spirit with freedom
and joy.
MAKE IT SO."

Here you may branch out and include any number of intentions
for healing, for blessings, for transformation. Make sure that
these follow the same format, that they are stated by decree and
in the present moment. When you are finished, make it clear
that you are complete by stating "Aho" or "Amen" or whatever
you are comfortable with.

Another prayer of great power is as follows:

"Inner Shaman, I instruct you to wake and activate all
my DNA, including all the physical elements and those
majority aspects that are quantum that I didn't know I
had access to."

Stop for a moment to feel, sense, or see the light spreading from
your heart to all your body and then to the entire luminous egg
around you from a radius of three feet to up to twenty-six feet
in its most expanded state. See the axis running through the top
of your head down through your perineum and below your feet.

"May every particle of my DNA be cleaned, activated, and made available to me to inform my body of its perfection and to inform me of the talents and capabilities I have not fully expressed thus far. Bring the information of X, Y, and Z forward that I may fully utilize it. DNA, I love you and honor you for being my access to the greater 'I AM.' Thank you, thank you, thank you."

Powerful prayers should never be rote, nor should they be done without feeling. The more feeling, intention, and willingness you put into them, the more power they have to make extraordinary changes in your life and the lives of those who surround you. One of my primary shamanic teachers, Guadalupe, told me, "When you pray, pray with tears." Pray each time as if your life depended on it, because it does.

At first, it is best to keep such prayers completely private. These are not for display. However, if you have a trusted community and you are called upon to lead a ceremony for them, you may adapt such a prayer for the greater good of all. You can start the same way, but eliminate the part about the shaman and simply do blessings instead.

13

THE INNER SHAMAN as BIG MEDICINE and HEALER

In the shamanic tradition, anything that helps someone is considered medicine for healing; this includes totems, plants, minerals, power places, ceremonies, events, and practically anything that can be named. Some highly evolved shamans say that everything is medicine. There are big medicines and small medicines—each is used depending on the need, the situation, and the time. For example, a shaman or a physician may prescribe plenty of fresh air or a trip to the mountains or the beach to support the health of a patient. This is considered medicine from the earth, powerful clean supportive energy for body and mind. When confronted with a child grieving over the loss of a pet, a shaman might prescribe a visit from a favorite relative, or a new puppy or kitten. In modern times, when people hear the word "medicine," they think of pharmaceuticals such as cough syrup or blood pressure medication, but in the shamanic understanding these may not be medicines at all but harmful agents with toxic effects on the body.

The Inner Shaman is big medicine with unlimited power and influence, able to be tapped at any time and in any place, by a shaman or directly by yourself. Totally natural and with enormous potential, the Inner Shaman supports not only physical health but emotional, mental, and spiritual balance as well. An adept is able to tap the Inner Shaman of anyone who comes to them for assistance. This is how great historical healers like Jesus were able to work what others took to be miracles. They were not limited by distance, time, or circumstances in their ministrations. A physical body pronounced dead is viable as long as the Inner Shaman is still present.

I have had numerous experiences with healing shamans who were able to cure me, members of my family, or participants in my groups of a temporary malady without pills, injections, or artificial chemicals. In many cases, they simply sang to the Inner Shaman, who then worked the necessary healing. This is why advanced shamans like my late Huichol teacher Guadalupe, and Shipibo teachers Enrique and the late Herlinda, never take credit for a healing but will always defer to Spirit. They know that their personality had nothing to do with the healing, that they were only a conduit for the Inner Shaman to bring back balance and harmony.

The Inner Shaman as Healer

As the Inner Shaman gazes out from your eyes, it is able to see the outward appearance of others as well as what is happening within them on more subtle levels. For example, you may notice that although someone appears normal externally, you can see or feel that they seem to be carrying the world on their back. You may see someone who appears cheerful on the outside, but you see, sense, or feel a great sadness inside. You may notice someone who appears confident, but is actually guarded and defensive. How can you know these things? This is harder to explain. The Inner Shaman simply knows, but also there may be clues. You may see a darkness in their chest or over their shoulders. You may read the uncertainty in their eyes, or simply match their feeling and sense that all is not well through what you begin to feel when you listen to them or spend time with them. You might receive pictures in your mind or simply know something about them that you could not know any other way. For example, you might see or sense that they were abused as a child or have been through an addictive process with alcohol or food disorders.

On a different level, you may sense that they are not going to live long, even though they seem perfectly healthy. Perhaps you sense that there is something wrong in their body even though they are unaware of it.

It is important to realize that you are not obligated to fix the condition nor is it always best to communicate it. This can be intrusive and inappropriate, given that you perhaps do not have the kind of relationship that would make telling them productive. The Inner Shaman may show you many things that you have to keep to yourself. If you do not want the responsibility of receiving this information, then you should reconsider whether to work with the Inner Shaman. On the other hand, you can ask the Inner Shaman to close off this information so that you are not privy to it. The Inner Shaman may not respond the way you want because it knows what you *need*, not what you want.

If you are already a healer or are in training to become one, what the Inner Shaman sees or senses in others can be very valuable to you. You can dialogue with the Inner Shaman, asking for clarification or for more specific information about what you sensed. You can also receive instruction about what you should say and how to say it, and what you should be circum-spect about. With practice, the Inner Shaman will also show you where to touch them, what to recommend to them, and so on. Make sure you always ask for permission before you do some-thing. For example, if the Inner Shaman tells you that placing your hand over their abdomen would be helpful, you must ask permission from the person first. You can say, "May I place my hand over your abdomen?" If they say no, you must respect that. Usually the promptings given to you by the Inner Shaman are well received by others, and they sense immediate relief. Occa-sionally there may be a more dramatic response, and they might burst into tears or howl. This can be disconcerting at first, but you must learn to expect it.

It is the Inner Shaman who is facilitating the healing. You have merely followed instructions, so there is no need to take credit. A dramatic response is not necessarily better than a sub-tle one. Sometimes great transformation happens quietly, with little fanfare. The Inner Shaman knows how to communicate with the other person, by thought, touch, or words, in a way that opens the door for them to heal themselves. That is the nature of true healing: all healing is self-healing. Most of the time, learning to facilitate healing is learning how to get out of the way. The most effective healing is minimalist. There is no need to brandish big healing tools, crystals, or the like. However, if you are instructed by the Inner Shaman to use such tools, then it would be best to do so.

Often the Inner Shaman will give you a song to sing to the other person. It will start with the mere hint of a melody. You may find yourself starting to whistle under your breath or tap-ping your fingers or foot to some inner beat or rhythm. Perhaps there will be a word that is repeated, or a simple phrase, but more often it is simply a sound, a rhythm, or a melody. Shamans call this catching a song. The songs are all around us all the time. They are part of the patterns that make up our universe. Like radio waves, just because you cannot see them does not mean they're not there. The Shipibos believe that the universe is always singing itself into being.

Do not refrain from exploring this sound and singing it or whistling it softly in the other's presence. Your ordinary personality may have no clue as to the power and transformative influence of this slight sound. If you are too busy feeling silly or self-conscious, you may deprive that other person of exactly what they need to begin a powerful healing process. Again, it is best to get yourself out of the way and do what the Inner Shaman prompts or urges you to do.

"Urge" is an important word here. The Inner Shaman often expresses itself in urges that seem to come from nowhere or everywhere. The urge will grow stronger and repeat itself if the Inner Shaman is emphasizing something. Once I was having a conversation with a client whose spouse had recently died and who was still in denial about the great sadness he felt. The Inner Shaman kept repeating a strange phrase to me over and over. I finally found a way to say the phrase and he leapt out of his chair, crashed to the floor and sobbed uncontrollably for ten minutes or so. I was a bit shocked. Later, when he had calmed down, he told me that that had been his wife's favorite phrase. Hearing it helped him release the grief he was holding onto. If I hadn't said it, the grief might not have been tapped into and he would have remained blocked until another circumstance released it. I could have patted myself on the back and told myself how clever I was, but I knew that this came directly from the Inner Shaman and I was just following instructions. Yet I still felt very good about it because a healing had happened, and I can always celebrate that.

14

LEARNING to TURN LIFE OVER to the INNER SHAMAN

Most of us have been raised to believe that we must make good decisions so that we can steer the activities of our lives well. While this may make good psychological sense, let us explore it from another angle. When we make bad decisions that lead us into difficulty, we are following the guidance of the false personality. All you have to do is look around you: you will see many people who make bad decision after bad decision. We try to educate people to use good judgment, and this tends to work for the most part. What we don't notice is that we make better decisions and use good judgment in our lives when we are aligning with Spirit more and working from false personality less. This leads to a life in which many of our decisions are fairly decent. However, much depends on who is judging whether our decisions are good or not. Sometimes good judgment is considered to be marrying well or getting a high-paying job. Sometimes decisions that are aligned with Spirit are considered to be bad ones, because they may not please others or lead to success in the material world. So the whole idea of using good judgment is a flawed one. What the hell is good judgment anyway?

There is only one good solution to all this—but it may sound outrageous to you. The solution is to turn every detail of your life over to the Inner Shaman and forget about what you think you ought to do. Granted, this is advanced work, and it might sound counterintuitive, but if you want to really accelerate, shamanically speaking, this is what you must do.

How can you go about turning every detail of your life over to the Inner Shaman? What would this look like? It is not shirking your responsibility to give everything to the Inner Shaman to solve. Your local personality may have some problem-solving skills, and you may have developed experience that helps you use fairly good judgment, but you need a lot more than a high IQ to navigate this world. That should be obvious after watching the world economy melt down and the disastrous decisions of politicians. The world is so complex, and there are so many variables, that even the smartest person may be overwhelmed by a sudden challenge. Wouldn't it be better to seek the advice of a person with vast experience and consistent excellent solutions? Is that lazy? No—not as long as you continue to do your utmost on your own. The best policy then is to use all the talents that you have at your disposal while at the same time delegating the problem to the one who is vastly superior at solving everything. In other words, you work together. You no longer worry, because even though you don't know what the solution is you know you have the best team working on the situation.

The first thing to do is to open up the conversation with the Inner Shaman. You can ask the Inner Shaman if it wishes you to call it by a particular name, or you may simply address it as

Inner Shaman, blessed one, powerful one, holy one, or whatever you like. The conversation can go something like this:

"Inner Shaman, you have my best interest in mind at all times. You are much more knowledgeable than I am and you have access to the vast intelligence of the Great Spirit. You know the outcome of all events and can see a much bigger picture than I can. I make decisions based on the past, what I am afraid of, or what I think may be a good idea from where I sit, but in all truth I can't completely see where I am going and whether I am heading off a cliff. You can and do see all. Therefore I love you and completely trust you to always guide me in the best possible ways. However, I have not been in the habit of checking with you before I do something so I need clear direction. Give me clear signs about what direction to take and I will do so."

The next order of business is to get in the habit of asking the Inner Shaman about major courses of action. Is this upcoming trip to Brazil the right course of action? Then you must learn to listen—and I mean, really listen. Many people are in the habit of asking a pendulum, checking with the *I-Ching*, or doing muscle testing to get responses to such questions. The problem with these methods is that they are time-consuming and not always accurate because there may be subconscious contamination of the responses. The false personality controls large parts of the subconscious, and the subconscious controls the body much of the time.

On the other hand, the Inner Shaman is ruthless and clear. If you should not go to Brazil, it will tell you so. If you don't listen, your flight will be canceled, there will be torrential flooding, the meeting will be canceled, or something will transpire that makes it impossible for you to go. That is the Inner Shaman responding to you indirectly when you don't listen, and this wastes time and energy and can be annoying. In the long run, it is best to make such a sound connection with the Inner Shaman that it simply tells you through undeniable seeing, sensing, or feeling, "No, don't go. Stay here." Or, "By all means go."

Your biggest problem will be trust. You may say, "How can I trust something I can't see or feel and that is perhaps a figment of my imagination?" Fine, don't trust the Inner Shaman. After all, that is probably what you have been doing in your life until recently—though you may be a fortunate exception. Take the inevitable consequences of controlling everything yourself. Good luck! However, if you are like many folks, you have grown tired of struggling with poor decisions and the consequences of trying to dominate life by micromanaging. You have discovered that your method has not borne fruit other than anxiety and stress. Fortunately, you are not out of luck. The Inner Shaman awaits you patiently. It is always ready to step in any time you give it your permission to do so, and it will not fail you. However, it may send you in directions that test your trust and perhaps surprise you.

Let's say you run a business and pride yourself on being an upstanding citizen, a person that never consorts with riffraff. You are a paragon of ethics and integrity. Now, let us say that a known prostitute or gangster contacts you and wants a meeting with you. You are about to dismiss them outright when your Inner Shaman says, "Meet with them. It will be important." You are in a quandary, because the Inner Shaman has directed you to do something you would never ordinarily do. Yet you listen and arrange for the meeting. The prostitute or gangster tells you that she or he is your in-law from an early former marriage, someone you have completely lost track of. They tell you that your ex-spouse has passed away but left you an important message. This message is one of forgiveness and heals an old hurt. It has such an impact on you that you experience a kind of transformation and see things in a very different light.

If you had been self-righteous and not met with the sleazy messenger, this wonderful opportunity would have been lost. So, it is always best to follow the advice of the Inner Shaman, even if you feel resistance or don't understand it. You can ask for clarification, and then simply give it your best shot. History is filled with incidents where a life was saved or someone was rescued because a person had the courage to follow the Inner Shaman without question.

I once canceled a skydiving session because I received a very clear message from the Inner Shaman not to go. I felt somewhat embarrassed, and because I could not get hold of the instructor I left a message that I would explain later. I never got my chance. The instructor filled my spot with another student, and they were both killed when the chute and reserve chute did not open. If I had not canceled, I would have been killed instead.

15

THE INNER SHAMAN as POWERFUL CREATOR

Shamans have always been excellent at manifesting because learning how to rearrange reality is a significant part of their training. First of all, shamans know that life is a waking dream and that dreams can be rescripted, altered, and rearranged. If you think of life as fixed or as completely random, then you are at the mercy of either fate or chaos. Both perspectives lead to a victim mentality, which is not acceptable on the shamanic path. The shaman knows well that life is as you dream it. If you don't like what is in your focus, change your focus.

This is not as simple as it might appear, because of the constant dance between the false personality and the Inner Shaman. The false personality has the ability to coopt your thoughts and feelings, so you may focus on things that are not good for you or simply narcissistic or egocentric. Your focus brings them about, no matter whether you are obsessed with the thoughts or in resistance to them. The Inner Shaman is content to sit back until you have chosen to ignore the false personality. The reason that the Inner Shaman is better at creating than the false personality is that it does not have an axe to grind. It is neutral. Since the false personality is not neutral, it resists your attempt to escape its clutches and this in the end is its downfall. In the long run it will create what it fears most, losing out to the Inner Shaman. Do you see now why the Inner Shaman will always win in the end? Shamans know that even though you have free will to choose whatever you want, in the end you will choose the path of the Inner Shaman. So why waste time with games that lead nowhere? Why not buckle down to the task of awakening the Inner Shaman sooner rather than later? Once a novice shaman sees this with absolute clarity, the goal is in sight, and even though there may be slight setbacks and distractions, the shaman knows that embracing the Inner Shaman is inevitable. This shaman is down to just a few more lifetimes of service.

GETTING PRIORITIES STRAIGHT

I will now bring up something that you should know if you are interested in waking up your Inner Shaman. Once you embark on this journey, you cannot look back. My Huichol teacher Guadalupe used to say, "Once you choose the shamanic path in earnest, you can never really get away with what you once might have. You can still lie, cheat, steal, and be out of integrity in your relationships, but you will not let yourself get away with it as you once did. If you don't follow the path with integrity, you will pay and pay very dearly for your transgressions. No one else is going to be on your case for this. It will be you and you alone that holds your feet to the fire. To be out of integrity is like allowing a pack of thieves to rampage through your home. They will wreak terrible carnage." You could say that this got my attention! In the years since, I have discovered through my experience that he was absolutely right. I can no longer be sloppy with my approach to life.

Someone on the shamanic path cannot get away with creating life from a narcissistic perspective. Abuse your abilities and you will pay dearly. On the other hand, you will be better at manifesting than ever before. With that said, let us get back to the business of creating and manifesting a life that fulfills and satisfies you at the deepest levels.

GETTING WHAT YOU NEED

As you have seen, you must give permission and instructions to the Inner Shaman as to what you want help with and where you want to go. I am not talking about wishing for a new car or house, because Spirit does not care about these things, unlike what some popular books suggest. Spirit does not regard any physical object as real, so it ignores that which is not energetic in nature, that which does not resonate with what Spirit is interested in. What Spirit responds to are instructions or questions that make it clear you want help in aligning with Spirit, so an instruction that tells Spirit to provide you with the resources necessary to be what you wish to be is more constructive. If your desire is to express your highest visions through musical or artistic means, Spirit knows what resources it will take to accomplish your goal and will provide you with exactly that. It may or may not be a new car that you need to become successful at that endeavor. You would not have an important mission in life and then not find the means to accomplish it. When you meet blocks and obstacles, they are tests and challenges to make you stronger, not permanent deterrents to your endeavors.

The main thing is that you be clear about what you want. Wanting to be free of the manipulation of the false personality is a worthy goal. Wanting to be aligned with Spirit in everything is a highly respectable goal. Wanting to have Spirit direct your thoughts is excellent and achievable if you just speak the words.

CREATING SMALL THINGS

Even small things are achievable if Spirit regards them as a worthwhile intention that contributes to your overall path. Once, at the farmers market in Santa Fe, I saw a buffalo hide on display. A local Indian tribe was selling buffalo meat that had been ceremonially prepared, and they were selling the hide of one that had been sacrificed in the traditional way. I thought this would be an excellent thing to sit on during my meditations, especially during the winter months when the floor in my house gets quite cold. The problem was that at that time I did not have the considerable cash that the skin cost. So I talked to Spirit via the Inner Shaman and said, "Spirit, I would like to have that skin to support my meditation. If you think it is a good idea for me to have it then provide me the funds so that I can purchase it. I will need it soon or it will be sold to someone else." Then I let it go and forgot about it.

A few days later I received a letter from a foreign woman whom my wife and I had helped many years before. She and her husband had arrived from her homeland without a penny to her name and we put them up for about a month while helping them get established. The letter was accompanied by a check for a considerable sum of money. In it she apologized and said she was so desperate that she had stolen some money from us when she stayed with us and that she had felt guilty ever since. She had gone on to be quite successful in the United States and she was repaying it now with interest.

I immediately wrote back and told her I was very happy to hear from her and held nothing against her. I was truly amazed at the rapid workings of Spirit. The check was enough to cover the cost of the buffalo skin and then some. To this day I use it to meditate on, and it provides me unlimited pleasure and warmth. I am reminded of how I got it every time I sit on it, and I smile. This creative dream worked because it contributed to my overall vision: the buffalo skin was to help me meditate, and meditating was to help me on my shamanic path, and my shamanic path was to help me be a good spiritual teacher and help others to find their true paths. This is the kind of event that happens often when you work with the Inner Shaman regularly. Shamans say that synchronistic events and serendipity are powerful signs that you are on the right track in your life, and they always accompany a successful practice.

EXERCISE **CREATING WHAT YOU NEED**

1. Find a comfortable private spot and sit with your spine erect.

2. Activate the Inner Shaman as you have learned to do in earlier exercises.

3. Focus on something that would support your path. Everyone needs a safe place to live, good reliable transportation, good companionship, a decent income, satisfying work; these are all worthy goals.

4. Keeping this as your focus, imagine that what you desire is already so. See yourself enjoying it, being it, having it, and experiencing the benefits of it.

5. Select one of those images in your mind's eye and focus on it as if it were in front of you and you were watching yourself as a spectator. Feel the feelings of having that image be true.

6. Find a way to connect yourself with that you in the future. You can draw a line between your heart and your heart in the image, or you can connect at the navel or tan tien.

7. Be sure to notice the awakened Inner Shaman in your own chest and in the chest of your future self. Imagine that through your Inner Shaman you are able to absorb through your physical and quantum genes all the information you need to bring this about. Imagine great streams of light arriving from all dimensions, from the stars, from the cosmos, and pouring into the crown of your head, where it moves down to the connection between you and your future self and begins to transfer over to it.

8. Now see if you can suddenly be over there looking out from your future self's eyes experiencing the new creation.

9. Feel great gratitude in your heart for what has come to pass. Give thanks to the Inner Shaman for the wonderful gift.

10. Now pop back over to yourself in the now. Let go of the whole process and just relax. Take a deep breath and wiggle your fingers and toes. You are complete.

There are several important ingredients in this process. First, you are working with the activated and awakened Inner Shaman. Next, you are actively experiencing what you desire—this is key. You are feeling the strong emotions and pleasure that the object of your desire will bring. This intensity of feeling activates the quantum field. The next key to activating the quantum field is the use of the double that allows you to create two points of reference simultaneously, your present self and your future self. When you connect to your double through an important portal in your energy body, your heart or your tan tien, you are opening to the quantum field that contains all the information about everything in past, present, and future and bringing in this information through your crown and through your genes. You are sharing this information with your future self. Then you bring in strong gratitude. Then you come back to your original reference point and let it go. What is actually happening here is that the two points are becoming waves, the present one collapsing and the future one one arising to replace it with what you are asking for.

A shaman would see the future self as no more or less real than your present self. They are equals in your dream of reality. In other words, they are simultaneous experiences happening in slightly different time frames. A shaman knows that all time is simultaneous to the Inner Shaman. Through your genes, you have access to and communication with all parts of the universe all the time. They are the tools that all creatures use to connect with the great Inner Shaman; through this connection you receive the instruction manual for navigating your life. You know you are a human being, and how to be one, while a deer knows how to be a deer. Through the gene connection a human can also know what it is to be a deer, perhaps even see through a deer's eyes on occasion.

This is all to say that shamans know that everything is possible because everything is connected. This is what makes shamans excellent creators. Even so, most shamans live very modest lives because they don't see much purpose in piling up material wealth and possessions. They are much happier being of service.

16

THE INNER SHAMAN
and the INNER LEVELS
of the BODY

Around the physical body is an egg-shaped energy field, called the light body by New Age healers, the luminous egg by shamans, and the poqpo by Q'ero shamans from Peru. This field of light can extend outward anywhere from a few inches from the body to many feet. When the field is fully extended, it can reach a radius of twenty-six feet. The egg shape, in general, is a powerful symbol of fertility and power, and its structure has tremendous strength. The egg is related to the birth of all animals, whether gestation takes place inside the body or in an egg external to the body. Shamans say it is no accident that human beings are contained within the egg shape of their energy field, as if they were gestating and preparing for the even more powerful birth of all their shamanic abilities.

The luminous egg is filled with filaments of light, weblike tiny threads emanating primarily from the solar plexus region, or tan tien. These high-frequency, multidimensional filaments, called nadis by the Hindus, are the mostly invisible form of the physical nervous system, a subtle network that enables humans to perceive their dream and interact with it. For example, Toltec shamans are said to be able to climb up vertical rock faces and cliffs without using their hands, only the filaments in their luminous egg. Taoist shamans who practice martial arts are able to protect themselves from external attack by activating this network of light filaments, and can even knock down their opponents without actually touching them with hands or feet.

The ancient Hindu Vedas say there are 72,000 nadis in the body and within the luminous egg. Since they are microscopic, much finer than the threads of a spider's web, many of them can fit into a compact space. By communicating directly with the physical and quantum aspects of the DNA, the Inner Shaman is capable of directing and managing all 72,000 nadis, millions of times a second. Yet because of our tendency to fall asleep and disconnect from the Inner Shaman, the nadis often become contaminated with thought forms of lower amplitude. They can become toxic, and when they do, our experience of living is substantially lowered, leading to physical and emotional dysfunction. When you make contact with your Inner Shaman, it is important to give it permission to purify, correct, and balance the nadis by communicating with your DNA.

At any given moment, the Inner Shaman is in communication with all the subtle structures of your body. Each organ is built upon deeper structures, which have properties that are much more powerful than the properties of your outer organs. The deeper structures interact with their corresponding organs and in many cases influence them. Your brain is the physical manifestation of your mind, that which you use when you are not in a body. Your eyes are designed to see the physical world, but are also functioning at much more subtle levels. Typically the brain does not compute all that the subtle eyes are seeing until a person becomes a master. When you cast off your body at death, you will still be able to see using your inner sight and you will have a much greater range of perception than you do now. Likewise, your physical heart is the outward manifestation of an inner heart that is the actual magnet and radiator of love. The heart that Jesus points to in statues and pictures is not the physical heart so much as the inner heart that houses the Inner Shaman.

Another example is the pituitary gland, in your brow region. The hormones that your ordinary pituitary gland regulates are limited compared to the subtle hormones produced by your subtle or quantum pituitary gland, the one that cannot be seen by the bodily eye. The inner pituitary, much like the higher centers, has the ability to produce subtle hormones (higher octaves of hormones) that, when harnessed, allow the body to perform in magical ways. When people walk on hot coals or when shamans put hot coals in their mouths, they do not burn because subtle hormones are released that protect the body from intense heat. In the same fashion, Tibetan Buddhists trained to withstand extreme cold without any clothing have learned to release subtle hormones that produce inner heat. These hormones are the product of the activated inner pituitary. Other inner hormones are capable of healing the body instantly from cancerous tumors and malignant tissue. These are the hormones released when someone heals as if by magic after receiving a death sentence from their physician.

When certain inner hormones are consciously released, they rejuvenate the cells of the body so that aging vastly slows, allowing the body to live way beyond its supposed hundred-year span. Others allow the body to levitate or bilocate—supernatural abilities for which shamans are famous. These powerful inner hormones can be released through specific shamanic practices, but sometimes they are released naturally. One condition that makes their release possible is inspiration, or the emotion that accompanies faith. Recognition of the truth accomplishes much the same thing. Shamans who know how to raise the overall frequency in ceremonies, with or without plant medicines, are capable of creating an atmosphere in which many people together experience activation of their inner organs. This group event often facilitates the seemingly miraculous healing of one, several, or all of the participants. One of the most common ways a shaman raises the frequency in a ceremony is through the singing of sacred songs.

If they were properly understood, these kinds of events would no longer be considered superstition, or miracles. They are natural outcomes to natural processes.

Other emotional states that facilitate the activation of subtle hormones include gratitude, love, and awe. These three powerful states produce what can be metaphorically described as fertilizer for the Inner Shaman to blossom forth. The more one focuses on these three states of being, the more accelerated is the activation of subtle hormones and the awakening of the Inner Shaman. I cannot stress enough how effective and how important this is to personal shamanic transformation. Great saints and masters from all traditions spend most of their waking hours focused in these states.

I have had the good fortune to spend a great deal of my adult life with Huichol people. I have often hired them to assist me in building and landscaping projects at my home in Santa Fe and on the land nearby where I hold retreats, solos, and ceremonies. I have never seen a Huichol complain, even in extremely hot, cold, or inclement weather. They are cheerful, focused, and highly cooperative all the time. They are always grateful for whatever happens, very loving toward one another and to everyone, and seem genuinely amazed at the world around them. In other words, they are masters at gratitude, love, and awe. Although I have a doctorate and they are much less educated from the point of view of our society, they are my teachers in what is most important.

On many occasions I have had the opportunity to work with a psychic surgeon from the Philippines, and I have experienced major healing from his ministrations. I have also been able to watch him work on my wife and others, and could see his fingers and hands draw out the toxins, blood clots, tumors, calcifications, and malignant tissue through the skin. I had experienced stiffness and pain in my back and neck due to whiplash in an automobile accident a number of years before. He pulled out chunks of scar tissue and calcification, giving me pain-free mobility in my neck and spinal cord, movement that I have retained.

When I asked him how he had learned to do this work, he said simply that it was a gift from God. He said he could not teach it but could answer questions about the nature of the body. I learned a lot from him about how the body works. Later, I understood more about what he does by learning about the inner organs and their products. He is able to increase his frequency and thereby release subtle hormones that allow him to draw out, through the skin of the other person's body, unhealthy objects. It is a natural human ability that he has learned to tap via the Inner Shaman, whom he calls God. Like other capable shamans and healers, he is able to communicate with the DNA directly so that positive changes occur instantaneously.

He told me that he visualizes his fingers as magnets able to draw out what is not in harmony with the body. This is the same technique used by Shipibo shamans: they visualize a magnet on the tip of the tongue and, placing their mouth directly over the malady, they suck it out and then spit or vomit to get rid of it. Shamans everywhere on earth perform their own versions of extraction. This is the original surgery, before anyone got the idea to physically cut into the body. After shamanic extraction there is no need for the body to recover; only rest and water intake are required.

Shamans understand that the human body is capable of healing immediately once it is clear on the instructions. If the body does not receive clear, healthy directives, it will follow the dictates of the subconscious mind, which often gives directives expressing punishment for guilt and perceived wrong doing. According to shamans, this is often the reason for illness or accidents. Sometimes people fall ill because they have lost an essential part of themselves due to trauma, grief, or susto (fright). This requires a soul retrieval, something that shamans perform on every continent. They go on a search for the lost part, the inner child that ran away when the person was abused or hurt. They find it, gain its confidence, and ask it to return. Then they blow it back into the person. The fact that Western medicine does not do this accounts for so many failed treatments. You cannot just treat the body with medications; you must restore what has been lost. Restoring it restores physical or psychological health.

For shamans, time is not relevant to recovery. Recovery of the body happens as soon as the disharmony or lack of resonance is removed. The Shipibos see lack of harmony in the body as a tangled web surrounding an organ, choking it off or disconnecting it from the rest of the body. They catch a song or sing a traditional *icaro* (sacred song) that unravels the tangle, releasing the body part from its prison and confusion. They may use tobacco smoke or the ash from burned tobacco for the same purpose. I have personally experienced profound healings as the result of such ministrations. The results can be immediate, such as the cessation of a fever, a sore throat, or extreme pain.

Your Inner Shaman is capable of orchestrating such healings as soon as it knows you are ready and clear about your intention to heal. This means you have to clear out all hidden agendas or distorted motivations for being ill. If you are not sure what those motivations are, you can always ask the Inner Shaman to help you clear them out. The good news is that you do not always have to know everything to heal yourself. All you need is the clear intention and the willingness to ask for help.

EXERCISE **HEALING YOURSELF WITH**
THE HELP OF THE INNER SHAMAN

1. Choose a physical, emotional, or mental symptom that has been giving you trouble. Maybe you have been having trouble with headaches, are angry or grief-stricken over a broken relationship, or have been struggling with obsessive thoughts.

2. Be clear that you want help from the Inner Shaman to release you from the harshness of these symptoms.

3. Use your preferred method to deeply relax and let go. We have covered several methods in prior exercises. Lie on the ground or sit quietly and, using your breath, let go deeply.

4. Visualize the Inner Shaman in your chest and make a connection with it. There is no one right way to do this. It is your intention that counts.

5. You can say: "Inner Shaman, I have been having trouble with X. Please unravel the disharmony creating the symptoms and release me from them. If it is appropriate, show me the lesson behind this problem. If not, just clear it up. I know you are able to do this. Thank you for your help."

Notice the steps: identify the problem, deeply relax, activate the Inner Shaman, ask for help, then give thanks for the help that you know will be coming forth. This does not have to be complicated. Many people who have been healed in an instant say how easy it was.

Shamanic healing is a vast topic and here we have only touched the tip of the iceberg. Much knowledge of healing comes directly from the Inner Shaman. I have seen many people who, after gradually discovering the shamanic path, eventually go on to become proficient and dedicated healers, even if only as a sideline to what they do for a living. This is a natural outcome of studying with the Inner Shaman, and one of the seven main skills of the shamanic path: artist, storyteller, healer, ceremonialist, warrior, leader, and teacher-student.

17

ADVANCED WORK
with the INNER SHAMAN

Now that you have become acquainted with the Inner Shaman and have worked with it in introductory ways, you may be ready to do more advanced work. Why should you do advanced work? The simple answer is that you don't have to. The reality is that as you proceed on your journey toward self-realization and developing all your abilities and talents, more advanced work will call to you. That is the way of nature. A tree that finds the sunlight grows straight and tall more quickly than one in the shade.

All the shamans I have worked with over the years stress the importance of proceeding step by step. They are always on the watch for any tendency in themselves or others to become impatient, and they attempt to head it off before it can take hold. Remember that impatience is based on fear, the fear that perhaps there won't be enough time and you have to hurry or you will lose out somehow. Hurry is the enemy of the shaman, so even though healing or other positive results can be instantaneous, shamans emphasize building on the learning leading up to the present situation. If you relax, you are giving a vote of confidence to the Inner Shaman that everything will work out fine. It will. There is no rush. Impatience is a vote of no confidence in the Inner Shaman and interferes with any positive results.

One of my teachers, Enrique, a Shipibo healer and shaman, has told me over and over, *"Vas a sanar poco a poco,"* meaning, "You will heal little by little." Sometimes I have felt better immediately, and sometimes it takes a few days or more. Sometimes I learn quickly and sometimes more slowly. It is all good and it takes what it takes, no less and no more.

The exercises we are about to do here are advanced because they involve quite a bit of movement back and forth between the inner world and the outer world. If you attempt to do this too soon, you may stimulate a healing crisis that can make you very uncomfortable for a brief period of time. A healing crisis happens when you push yourself too far or too fast and stimulate a backlash, similar to the kind of unpleasant reaction you have if you work out too much on your first day. This is why shamans always suggest approaching *poco a poco*, little by little. They know you can experience overwhelming feelings, confusion, or even anxiety if you try to push yourself too hard, because the personality has resistance and will push back.

In these next exercises we are going to work with the vesica pisces, the fish-shaped entrance that shamans like to use for travel to other dimensions. As already discussed, this shape is a portal to the Tao or, as shamans refer to it, the Spirit World. The Christian association of Christ with the fish is for good reason: Jesus was well aware of this portal.

A Foot in Both Worlds

The classical shaman is believed to have a foot in both worlds, the material world and the Spirit World, and is able to cross back and forth at will to accomplish specific aims. What this actually means is that a shaman is able to change his or her perception from one dimension to another. However, shamans know that there are not really two worlds, but one. There is the material or substantial world, which is only a dream, and then there is the Spirit World—the world that is in fact real. The portal between what is real and what is not is in the shape of a vesica pisces. Sometimes it is seen as a cave entrance, a hole in a tree, a fissure in the ground, or a pool of water. As you pass through the portal, it is typical to feel a little resistance, as if you are going through a veil or membrane, like the stargate represented in a popular television series and movie. I remember as a child I would often get stuck in this membrane when I had a high fever and was delirious. The membrane showed up as a thick rubbery substance with thousands of black and white specks all over it. I have heard others describe it in a similar way. Subsequently I learned that I needed a little momentum created by my strong intention to cross this membrane. I also learned about the need to establish a vesica pisces to be able to cross the membrane.

The fish's shape, which is similar to that of an aircraft's wing, allows the fish to travel through the water at amazing speed. The air or water is forced over a widened area and then collapses back together, propelling the craft forward and up. Even more importantly, this shape allows certain fish, such as salmon, to travel up the most difficult waterfalls and rapids in order to reach their spawning grounds. For shamans, the fish shape is one of the secrets to intradimensional travel.

EXERCISE **CONTEMPLATION ON THE INNER SHAMAN**

1. Take a moment to imagine the Inner Shaman, sitting on a seat or standing within the vesica pisces formed around your heart.

2. Once you have your Inner Shaman in mind, imagine that you are looking outward through the Inner Shaman's eyes, sitting or standing in the portal formed by the vesica pisces.

3. Move forward through the portal and feel the slight resistance of the membrane. In the outside world in front of your chest, you experience the physical world, where all the emotions generated by the ego seem to exist. It can feel like a tempest of emotion: sadness, anger, envy, spite, excitement, and so on.

4. Step backward through the portal and once again feel the slight impact of the membrane between the two worlds. When you move back into the Spirit World, you experience freedom from all things generated by the ego, which lead to separation. Here, within the form of the Inner Shaman, you experience ecstasy, bliss, and unity. This does not mean that you should remain inside and resist stepping forward to the outer world. That is where the work lies. When you connect with the Inner Shaman and then step forward, you can do the most good because you bring the power of the Spirit World into the everyday world of apparent separation.

5. Continue to step back and forth through this portal, experiencing the difference between being on the

inside and being on the outside of your body, always occupying the form of the Inner Shaman.

6. Now take a rest.

At first glance, the next exercise may seem to duplicate the previous one. Although they have similarities, they are not the same. One builds to the next.

EXERCISE **CONTEMPLATING THE WORLD OF IDENTIFICATION**

First, read this contemplation through. When you understand the basic movement, close your eyes and do it without reading.

1. Begin by imagining that you have your focused attention just in front of your chest and you are looking right at it. You are facing the portal leading to the Inner Shaman, the portal you stepped through during the last exercise. In this exercise, you are beginning on the outside, and your Inner Shaman is inside the body.

2. Allow yourself to feel the currents of moods and emotions associated with various thoughts. Do not avoid or resist what you think and feel.

3. Notice that while these emotions and sensations seem to be associated with your storyline—in other words, memories, experiences, or thoughts—the emotions exist independently of them. They only appear to be caused by the stimuli of your story. Actually they are free-floating emotions generated by the ego, looking for thoughts to attach to and then eventually to manifest into events.

4. Examine them as if you were examining a strange insect. See the truth about what they are: for example, that the sadness is not really your sadness, it is just sadness, nor is it related to what you thought was a sad thought or event. Similarly, anger and excitement are free-floating artifacts of the false personality—the grand ego of all humanity, not just yours. These feelings are drifting along looking for a home. The minute you lock onto them by identifying with the feeling, they find a temporary home. By observing them, you are not locking onto them.

5. Move forward and enter the portal. Approach the Inner Shaman. Feel yourself surrounded by the most brilliant, beautiful light. It may have hints of gold, of pink, and of electric blue, or it may be the brightest crystalline radiance.

6. Notice what has happened to the emotions and sensations of the ego you brought with you from the outer world. Could they come with you into this inner space?

7. Take a deep breath and feel yourself sigh. Allow yourself to receive and absorb the beautiful light and feel how it raises your amplitude. Let yourself commune with any allies or spirits that occupy this light space that appears to be in your chest. Let them teach you, inform you, heal you, and gift you.

8. Now, move yourself back out, with all you have received, through the vesica pisces portal back

to the dream of the material world, the world of separation. Notice how you are fortified, strengthened, renewed, refreshed, revitalized, refined, restored, and rejuvenated.

9. Explore this simple movement back and forth through the vesica pisces portal. Become adept at this activity. Spend a little time in each space and allow yourself to experience what it is like to drag the experience of the Spirit World into the world of substance again and again. Each time, pay attention to the shape of the vesica pisces and observe exactly what happens as you pass through it.

These two exercises are a tiny fraction of what is available to you as you begin to work with the Inner Shaman on a daily basis. The key is consistency and daily practice. You need not spend hours doing these practices. Even a few minutes a day will make a difference. The best approach is acknowledging and exercising the Inner Shaman several times a day for a few minutes each time. This makes it a regular part of your day, and when you miss a day you will feel the absence of your practice. I will give you some examples of how I work with it.

Since I am a psychotherapist, consultant, and coach by trade, I have the opportunity to take a minute before each session, during which I address the Inner Shaman. I invite it to be fully present during the session, to oversee the conversation, and to direct me in the ways most favorable to the client. At the end, I give thanks for the help. I have had the opportunity to compare the quality of my sessions with people when I remember to invite the Inner Shaman and when I forget. There is a huge difference. Needless to say, I do the same procedure when I start a class, lecture, seminar, or retreat.

It is important to be not simply a taker, but to also give back. This is the concept of *ayni* that I learned from the Q'ero shamans. For them, everything requires reciprocation: if you receive something, you must give back, even if it is only thanks. This keeps balance in the universe, and when it is practiced, everything runs smoothly. Thanking the Inner Shaman is the least you can do, but it is good to do more. Every morning I offer tobacco to the Inner Shaman for the help I have been given and am about to receive. On occasion I will have a little fire ceremony, where I burn copal and incense or sage and thank the Inner Shaman in a deeper way. If that is not possible, simply lighting a candle on a little altar devoted to the practice is a nice thing to do. The Inner Shaman does not demand anything in return. The reason for giving thanks is that it helps me keep the proper perspective and reminds me not to take anything for granted.

Sometimes the Inner Shaman takes these opportunities to teach me something or to give me advice. Sometimes it gives me suggestions for things I can do to make my practice better. At these times, my job is simply to listen.

I am not saying you need to do these exact things. I do suggest you find your own way to integrate the Inner Shaman into your life. Remember that you do not even have to call it the Inner Shaman. You can call it anything you want, as long as you keep the spirit of the practice in mind. I know one person who prefers to call this inner help Isis, and another who calls it Essence. Choose what is most meaningful to you.

THE BIG PORTAL is OPENING; HELP is HERE

The time is ripe. For this reason, information about the Inner Shaman is poised to become vastly more widespread. The information may use a variety of terminologies and call the Inner Shaman by other names. This does not matter at all. These age-old ideas are the next phase of development and growth for all humanity. It is the species' destiny to wake up to the power of the Inner Shaman, because that is the purpose of the game we are playing. It is what we have always wanted: to remember who we really are and wake up. It is your destiny, sooner or later—not your fate. A destiny you choose; a fate you do not.

Shamanically speaking, all biological experiments on all inhabited planets are ultimately doomed to failure without the guidance of the Inner Shaman to light their way. Without it, the life forms are simply too primitive, lacking in the essential knowledge of where they are going and what they are capable of. Not all the experiments in consciousness on different planets are successful each time. If the sentient life forms never discover the Inner Shaman, then their experiment is over. The species does not thrive. Ultimately this is not a problem, because experiments in consciousness are repeated over and over until they do succeed, no matter how long it takes.

This planet is no different. Our scientists have discovered many things through their experiments and research, but there are limits to how far they can go. If we as a species fail to take into consideration the spiritual element, we will produce unfortunate results—as we have already begun to do. A species cannot evolve to the highest levels by denying the source of its power. When scientific experiments produce good results, there is some element of conscious awareness and cooperation or resonance with Spirit. The older a soul the scientist is, the more truthful and beneficial the results of the experiment.

To make the quantum leap to our next levels of evolution, we will have to acknowledge and consult with the Inner Shaman. There is no other way. Shamans say there are a great many spectators watching this critical transition time on the earth. Will we make the leap? I believe we will. I can feel it, sense it. This is not a result of rational thought. It is a knowing. The time has come for us to grow up and leave childhood behind. There are those who are reluctant. That is okay. Even more are embracing maturity. That is wonderful.

There is one more thing you should know. Because it is time, inventors are downloading various new technologies that are capable of communicating with your body's gene pool, that work with your body at the highest-level frequencies, that speak the language of the Inner Shaman. This is another way that the Inner Shaman and your genes can become activated to provide a much larger service. Technologies such as Holosync, the quantum styli, and various computer programs that work with the quantum field are part of this new set of technologies. Other new technologies do not require physical products at all. They are simply revisited ancient techniques that involve using your hands, your voice, and your intention to manipulate the quantum field. Many more of these approaches are coming. What you need to know is that these technologies are vastly more effective if they are paired with direct communication with your Inner Shaman or directly with your genes. If you use these technologies without awakening your Inner Shaman, without communicating with your genes, without using the power of your words, the effects may be minimal and you may decide that they don't work. That would be a shame. This is like not understanding how to use new software for your computer and dumping a perfectly good program in the trash.

Of course, you don't have to use these powerful new software bundles. You can do things the same as you always have and struggle along, manipulating and controlling out of fear, micro-managing, judging, and punishing, but don't expect new results. It's up to you.

Ultimately there is no right way, but there are easier ways to live. You can discover them by tapping into the powers of the Inner Shaman and using the higher centers, the higher aspects of your emotional center, intellectual center, and moving center. Have fun and talk to your genes often, every day. Expect good results, but give them a little time to awaken. Once the results start they won't stop, and you will be in for a great ride. Then share with others. Happy trails to you and many, many blessings.

Much Love,
José Luis Stevens

BIBLIOGRAPHY

The primary information about the Inner Shaman I learned from direct experience. Listed below are books that have been influential on my journey.

Adyashanti. *The Impact of Awakening.* Los Gatos, CA: Open Gate Publishing, 2000.

Aribalo, Mallku. *Inka Power Places.* Cusco, Peru: Shamanic Productions, 2007.

Arrien, Angeles. *The Fourfold Way: Walking the Paths of the Warrior, Teacher, Healer and Visionary.* New York: HarperCollins, 1993.

Audlin, James David (Distant Eagle). *Circle of Life: Traditional Teachings of Native American Elders.* Santa Fe: Clear Light, 2006.

Avila, Elena. *Woman Who Glows in the Dark: A Curandera Reveals Traditional Secrets of Physical and Spiritual Health.* New York: Tarcher, 2000.

Bartlett, Richard. *The Physics of Miracles: Tapping into the Field of Consciousness Potential.* New York: Atria, 2009.

Bear, Jaya. *Amazon Magic: The Life Story of Ayahuasquero and Shaman Don Agustin Rivas Vasquez.* Taos, NM: Colibri, 2000.

Braden, Gregg. *The God Code.* Carlsbad, CA: Hay House, 2004.

———. *Walking Between the Worlds: The Science of Compassion.* Bellevue, WA: Radio Bookstore Press, 1997.

Brown, Tom, Jr. *The Journey.* New York: Berkley Books, 1992.

Buhner, Stephen Harrod. *The Secret Teachings of Plants.* Rochester, VT: Bear and Company, 2004.

Bynum, Edward. *The African Unconscious: Roots of Ancient Mysticism and Modern Psychology.* New York: Columbia University/ Teacher's College Press, 1999.

Calvo, César. *The Three Halves of Ino Moxo: Teachings of the Wizard of the Upper Amazon.* Translated by Ken Symington. Rochester, VT: Inner Traditions, 1995.

Carroll, Lee. *The Twelve Layers of DNA: An Esoteric Study of the Mastery Within.* Sedona, AZ: Platinum, 2010.

Castaneda, Carlos. *The Active Side of Infinity.* New York: HarperCollins, 1998.

———. *The Art of Dreaming.* New York: HarperCollins, 1993.

———. *The Eagle's Gift.* New York: Simon and Schuster, 1981.

———. *The Fire from Within.* New York: Simon and Schuster, 1984.

———. *Journey to Ixtlan: The Lessons of Don Juan.* New York: Simon and Schuster, 1972.

———. *Magical Passes: The Practical Wisdom of the Shamans of Ancient Mexico.* New York: HarperCollins, 1998.

———. *The Power of Silence: Further Lessons of Don Juan.* New York: Simon and Schuster, 1987.

———. *A Separate Reality: Further Conversations with Don Juan.* New York: Simon and Schuster, 1971.

———. *Tales of Power.* New York: Simon and Schuster, 1974.

———. *The Teachings of Don Juan: A Yaqui Way of Knowledge.* Berkeley: University of California Press, 1968.

———. *The Wheel of Time: The Shamans of Ancient Mexico, Their Thoughts about Life, Death and the Universe.* New York: Washington Square Press, 1998.

Chatwin, Bruce. *The Songlines.* New York: Viking, 1987.

Chopra, Deepak. *Creating Affluence: Wealth Consciousness in the Field of All Possibilities.* Novato, CA: New World Library, 1993.

———. *Life After Death: The Burden of Proof.* New York: Three Rivers Press, 2006.

———. *The Spontaneous Fulfillment of Desire: Harnessing the Infinite Power of Coincidence.* New York: Harmony, 2003.

Clow, Barbara. *Alchemy of the Nine Dimensions: Decoding the Vertical Axis, Crop Circles, and the Mayan Calendar.* Charlottesville, VA: Hampton Roads, 2004.

Cook, Pat. *Shaman, Jhankri, and Nele: Music Healers of Indigenous Cultures.* Roslyn, NY: Ellipsis Arts, 1997.

Cowan, Eliot. *Plant Spirit Medicine: The Healing Power of Plants.* Columbus, NC: Swan Raven, 1995.

Dobkin De Rios, Marlene. *Amazon Healer: The Life and Times of an Urban Shaman.* Bridport, UK: Prism Press, 1992.

Donner, Florinda. *Being-In-Dreaming: An Initiation into the Sorcerer's World.* New York: HarperCollins, 1991.

Eagle Feather, Ken. *A Toltec Path.* Charlottesville, VA: Hampton Roads, 1995.

Eaton, Evelyn. *The Shaman and the Medicine Wheel.* Wheaton, IL: Theosophical Publishing, 1982.

Eliade, Mircea. *Shamanism: Archaic Techniques of Ecstasy.* Princeton: Princeton University Press, 1964.

Elkin, A. P. *Aboriginal Men of High Degree: Initiation and Sorcery in the World's Oldest Tradition.* Rochester, VT: Inner Traditions, 1994.

Endredy, James. *Earthwalks for Body and Spirit: Exercises to Restore Our Sacred Bond with the Earth.* Rochester, VT: Bear and Company, 2002.

Espinoza, Luis. *Chamalú: The Shamanic Way of the Heart: Traditional Teachings from the Andes.* Rochester, VT: Destiny Books, 1995.

Falco, Howard. *I AM: The Power of Discovering Who You Really Are.* New York: Tarcher, 2010.

Forest, Ohky Simone. *Dreaming the Council Ways: True Native Teachings from the Red Lodge.* York Beach, ME: Samuel Weiser, 2000.

Foundation for Inner Peace. *A Course In Miracles.* Combined volume. Mill Valley, CA: Foundation for Inner Peace, 2007.

Govindan, Marshall. *Kriya Yoga Sutras of Patanjali and the Siddhas.* Eastman, Quebec: Kriya Yoga Publications, 2000.

Grim, John. *The Shaman: Patterns of Religious Healing Among the Ojibway Indians.* Norman: University of Oklahoma Press, 1983.

Halifax, Joan. *Shamanic Voices: A Survey of Visionary Narratives.* New York: Dutton, 1979.

Harner, Michael. *The Way of the Shaman: A Guide to Power and Healing.* New York: HarperCollins, 1980.

Harris, Bill. *Managing Evolutionary Growth: How to Create Deep Change Without Falling Apart.* Beaverton, OR: Centrepoint Research Institute, 2007.

———. *Thresholds of the Mind.* Beaverton, OR: Centrepoint Research Institute, 2007.

Hawking, Stephen, and Leonard Mlodinow. *The Grand Design.* New York: Bantam, 2010.

Heaven, Ross, and Howard Charing. *Plant Spirit Shamanism: Traditional Techniques for Healing the Soul.* Rochester, VT: Destiny Books, 2006.

Hirschi, Gertrud. *Mudras: Yoga in Your Hands.* York Beach, ME: Samuel Weiser, 2000.

Ingerman, Sandra. *Medicine for the Earth: How to Transform Personal and Environmental Toxins.* New York: Three Rivers Press, 2000.

———. *Soul Retrieval: Mending the Fragmented Self.* New York: HarperCollins, 1991.

———, and Hank Wesselman. *Awakening to the Spirit World: The Shamanic Path of Direct Revelation.* Boulder, CO: Sounds True, 2010. [Includes sections by José Luis Stevens]

Jenkins, Elizabeth. *Initiation: A Woman's Spiritual Adventure in the Heart of the Andes.* New York: Putnam, 1997.

Jones, Blackwolf, and Gina Jones. *Listen to the Drum: Blackwolf Shares His Medicine.* Center City, MN: Hazelden, 1995.

Kaiguo, Chen, and Zheng Shunchao. *Opening the Dragon Gate: The Making of a Modern Taoist Wizard.* Translated by Thomas Cleary. Boston: Charles Tuttle, 1998.

Kakar, Sudhir. *Shamans, Mystics, and Doctors: A Psychological Inquiry into India and Its Healing Traditions.* New York: Knopf, 1982.

Katz, Richard. *Boiling Energy: Community Healing among the Kalahari Kung.* Cambridge, MA: Harvard University Press, 1982.

Kenyon, Tom. *Brain States.* Lithia Springs, GA: World Tree Press, 2001.

————, and Judi Sion. *The Magdalen Manuscript: The Alchemies of Horus and the Sex Magic of Isis.* Boulder, CO: Sounds True, 2006.

Kharitidi, Olga. *Entering the Circle.* Albuquerque: Gloria Press, 1995.

Kim, Tae Yun. *Seven Steps to Inner Power.* Novato, CA: New World Library, 1991.

————. *The Silent Master: Awakening the Power Within.* Novato, CA: New World Library, 1994.

Lajo, Javier. *Qhapaq Nan: The Inka Path of Wisdom.* Lima, Peru: Amaro Runa Ediciones, 2007.

Lamb, F. Bruce. *Rio Tigre and Beyond.* Berkeley, CA: North Atlantic Books, 1985.

Langford, Michael. *The Most Direct and Rapid Means to Eternal Bliss.* Freedom Religion Press, 2007.

Larsen, Stephen. *The Shaman's Doorway.* New York: Harper and Row, 1976.

Magee, Matthew. *Peruvian Shamanism: The Pachakuti Mesa.* Black Mountain, NC: Heart of the Healer, 2002.

Maharaj, Sri Nisargadatta. *I Am That: Talks with Sri Nisargadatta Maharaj.* Dunham, NC: Acorn Press, 2005.

Marciniak, Barbara. *Path of Empowerment: Pleiadian Wisdom for a World in Chaos.* San Francisco: Inner Ocean, 2004.

Mares, Theun. *Return of the Warriors: The Toltec Teachings.* Volume 1, *Revealing the Ancient Mystery of Atl: A Path of Freedom, Joy, and Power.* Cape Town: Lion Heart, 1995.

Matthews, John. *The Celtic Shaman: A Handbook.* Rockport, MA: Element, 1991.

McCraty, R. "The Energetic Heart: Bioelectromagnetic Communication Within and Between People." In *Bioelectromagnetic Medicine,* edited by P. J. Rosch and M. S. Markov. New York: Marcel Dekker, 2004: 511–32.

————. "Influence of Cardiac Afferent Input on Heart–Brain Synchronization and Cognitive Performance." *International Journal of Psychophysiology* 45, no. 1–2 (2002): 72–73.

—————. "Psychophysiological Coherence: A Link Between Positive Emotions, Stress Reduction, Performance and Health." *Proceedings of the Eleventh International Congress on Stress, Mauna Lani Bay, HI, 2000.*

—————, M. Atkinson, and R. T. Bradley. "Electrophysiological Evidence of Intuition: Part 1. The Surprising Role of the Heart." *Journal of Alternative and Complementary Medicine* 10, no. 1 (2004): 133–43.

—————, M. Atkinson, and R. T. Bradley. "Electrophysiological Evidence of Intuition. Part 2: A System-Wide Process?" *Journal of Alternative and Complementary Medicine* 10, no. 2 (2004): 325–36.

—————, M. Atkinson, W. A. Tiller, et al. "The Effects of Emotions on Short-Term Power Spectrum Analysis of Heart Rate Variability." *American Journal of Cardiology* 76, no. 14 (1995): 1089–93.

—————, R. T. Bradley, and D. Tomasino. "The Resonant Heart." *Shift: At the Frontiers of Consciousness* 5 (2004): 15–19.

Melchizedek, Drunvalo. *The Ancient Secret of the Flower of Life.* 2 vols. Flagstaff, AZ: Light Technology, 2000.

—————. *Living in the Heart: How to Enter into the Sacred Space within the Heart.* Flagstaff, AZ: Light Technology, 2003.

—————. *Serpent of Light: Beyond 2012.* San Francisco: Samuel Weiser, 2007.

Metzner, Ralph. *Ayahuasca: Consciousness and the Human Spirit of Nature.* New York: Thunder's Mouth Press, 1999.

Mindell, Arnold. *The Shaman's Body: A New Shamanism for Transforming Health, Relationships, and the Community.* New York: HarperCollins, 1993.

Ming-Dao, Deng. *Everyday Tao: Living with Balance and Harmony.* New York: HarperCollins, 1996.

—————. *Scholar Warrior: An Introduction to the Tao in Everyday Life.* New York: HarperCollins, 1990.

Montgomery, Pam. *Plant Spirit Healing: A Guide to Working with Plant Consciousness.* Rochester, VT: Bear and Company, 2008.

Moss, Nan, with David Corbin. *Weather Shamanism: Harmonizing Our Connection with the Elements.* Rochester, VT: Bear and Company, 2008.

Narby, Jeremy. *The Cosmic Serpent: DNA and the Origins of Knowledge*. New York: Tarcher, 1998.

———, and Francis Huxley, eds. *Shamans Through Time: 500 Years on the Path to Knowledge*. New York: Tarcher, 2001.

Nelson, Mary, and Don Miguel Ruiz. *Beyond Fear: A Toltec Guide to Freedom and Joy*. Tulsa: Council Oak Books, 1997.

Nicholson, Shirley. *Shamanism*. Wheaton, IL: Theosophical Publishing House, 1987.

Nowak, Margaret, and Stephen Durrant. *The Tale of a Nisan Shamaness: A Manchu Folk Epic*. Seattle: University of Washington Press, 1977.

Opler, Morris Edward. *An Apache Life-Way: The Economic, Social, and Religious Institutions of the Chiricahua Indians*. Lincoln: University of Nebraska Press, 1996.

Orieux, Jean. *Talleyrand: The Art of Survival*. Translated by Patricia Wolf. New York: Knopf, 1974.

Parker, K. Langloh. *Wise Women of the Dreamtime*. Rochester, VT: Inner Traditions, 1993.

Perkins, John. *The World as You Dream It: Shamanic Teachings from the Amazon and Andes*. Rochester, VT: Destiny Books, 1994.

Perry, Foster. *The Violet Forest: Shamanic Journeys in the Amazon*. Santa Fe: Bear and Company, 1998.

Pinchbeck, Daniel. *Breaking Open the Head: A Psychedelic Journey into the Heart of Contemporary Shamanism*. New York: Broadway Books, 2002.

Pinkson, Tom Soloway. *The Flowers of Wiricuta: A Journey to Shamanic Power with the Huichol Indians of Mexico*. Rochester, VT: Destiny Books, 1995.

Proceedings of the Third International Conference on the Study of Shamanism and Alternate Modes of Healing: Independent Scholars of Asia, 1986.

Proceedings of the Fourth International Conference on the Study of Shamanism and Alternate Modes of Healing: Independent Scholars of Asia, 1987.

Proceedings of the Fifth International Conference on the Study of Shamanism and Alternate Modes of Healing: Independent Scholars of Asia, 1988.

Proceedings of the Sixth International Conference on the Study
of Shamanism and Alternate Modes of Healing: Independent
Scholars of Asia, 1989.

Proceedings of the Seventh International Conference on the Study
of Shamanism and Alternate Modes of Healing: Independent
Scholars of Asia, 1990.

Reinhard, Johan. *Machu Picchu: The Sacred Center*. Lima, Peru:
Nuevas Imagenes, 1991.

Rinpoche, Tenzin Wangyal. *Healing with Form, Energy and Light:
The Five Elements in Tibetan Shamansim, Tantra, and Dzogchen*.
Ithaca, NY, and Boulder, CO: Snow Lion, 2002.

Roads, Michael J. *Talking with Nature*. Tiburon, CA: Kramer, 1985.

Ruiz, Miguel. *The Four Agreements: A Practical Guide to Personal
Freedom*. San Rafael, CA: Amber-Allen, 1997.

———. *The Mastery of Love: A Practical Guide to the Art of
Relationship*. San Rafael, CA: Amber-Allen, 1999.

———. *The Voice of Knowledge: A Practical Guide to Inner Peace*. San
Rafael, CA: Amber-Allen, 2004.

Sanchez, Victor. *The Teachings of Don Carlos: Practical Applications
of the Works of Carlos Castaneda*. Translated by Robert Nelson.
Santa Fe: Bear and Company, 1995.

———. *The Toltec Path of Recapitulation*. Rochester, VT: Bear and
Company, 2001.

———. *Toltecs of the New Millennium*. Translated by Robert Nelson.
Santa Fe: Bear and Company, 1996.

Sarangerel. *Riding Windhorses: A Journey into the Heart of Mongolian
Shamanism*. Rochester, VT: Destiny Books, 2000.

Schaefer, Stacy, and Peter Furst, eds. *People of the Peyote: Huichol
Indian History, Religion, and Survival*. Albuquerque: University
of New Mexico Press, 1996.

Schultes, Richard Evans, and Robert Raffauf. *Vine of the Soul:
Medicine Men, Their Plants and Rituals in the Colombian
Amazonia*. Santa Fe: Synergetic Press, 2004.

Selig, Paul. *I Am The Word: A Guide to the Consciousness of Man's Self
in a Transitioning Time*. New York: Tarcher, 2010.

Somé, Malidoma Patrice. *Of Water and the Spirit: Ritual, Magic, and Initiation in the Life of an African Shaman.* New York: Penguin, 1994.

———. *Ritual: Power, Healing, and Community.* Portland, OR: Swan Raven, 1993.

Somé, Sobonfu. *The Spirit of Intimacy: Ancient African Teachings in the Ways of Relationship.* New York: Morrow, 2000.

Spalding, Baird. *Life and Teaching of the Masters of the Far East.* 6 vols. Camarillo, CA: De Vorss, 1972.

Tacey, David. *Edge of the Sacred: Transformation in Australia.* North Blackburn, Victoria, Australia: HarperCollins, 1995.

Villoldo, Alberto, and Erik Jendresen. *Dance of the Four Winds: Secrets of the Inca Medicine Wheel.* Rochester, VT: Destiny Books, 1990.

———. *Island of the Sun: Mastering the Inca Medicine Wheel.* Rochester, VT: Destiny Books, 1992.

Vitebsky, Piers. *The Shaman: Voyages of the Soul, Trance, Ecstasy, and Healing from Siberia to the Amazon.* New York: Little Brown, 1995.

Weiskopf, Jimmy. *Yaje, the New Purgatory: Encounters with Ayahuasca.* Bogotá: Villegas Editores, 2004.

Whitaker, Kay Cordell. *The Reluctant Shaman: A Woman's First Encounter with the Unseen Spirits of the Earth.* New York: HarperCollins, 1991.

Whitley, David. *Following the Shaman's Path.* Ridgecrest, CA: Maturango Museum Press, 1998.

Wilcox, Joan Parisi. *Ayahuasca: The Visionary and Healing Powers of the Vine of the Soul.* Rochester, VT: Park Street Press, 2003.

———. *Masters of the Living Energy: The Mystical World of the Q'ero in Peru.* Rochester, VT: Inner Traditions, 2004.

Wildish, Paul. *Principles of Taoism.* London: HarperCollins, 2000.

Williams, J. E. *The Andean Codex: Adventures and Initiations among the Peruvian Shamans.* Charlottesville, VA: Hampton Roads, 2005.

Wong, Eva, trans. *Seven Taoist Masters: A Folk Novel of China.* Boston: Shambala, 1990.

Yogananda, Paramahansa. *The Yoga of Jesus.* Los Angeles: Self Realization Fellowship, 2007.

Zink, Nelson. *The Structure of Delight.* Santa Fe: Mind Matters, 1991.

By José Luis Stevens

Earth to Tao: Michael's Guide to Healing and Spiritual Growth. Santa
Fe: Bear and Company, 1994.

The Power Path: The Shaman's Way to Success in Business and Life.
Novato, CA: New World Library, 2002.

*Praying with Power: How to Use Ancient Shamanic Techniques to Gain
Maximum Spiritual Benefit and Extraordinary Results Through
Prayer.* London: Watkins, 2005.

Secrets of Shamanism: Tapping the Spirit Power Within You. New York:
Avon, 1988. [With Lena Stevens.]

Tao to Earth: Michael's Guide to Relationships and Growth. Santa Fe:
Bear and Company, 1994.

Transforming Your Dragons: Turning Fear Patterns into Personal Power.
Santa Fe: Bear and Company, 1994.

Ingerman, Sandra and Hank Wesselman. *Awakening to the Spirit
World: The Shamanic Path of Direct Revelation.* Boulder, CO:
Sounds True, 2010. [Includes sections by José Luis Stevens.]

E-Book Series: The Personessence System
for Understanding People (2010)

1. *Introduction to the Personessence System*
2. *The Seven Archetypal Roles: Primary Way of Being*
3. *The Seven Goals and the Seven Modes: Primary
   Motivation and Primary Approach*
4. *The Seven Attitudes: Primary Perspective*
5. *The Seven Obstacles: Primary Fear Pattern*
6. *The Seven Centers: Primary Reaction Centers*
7. *The Nine Needs: Primary Requirements for Balance*
8. *The Seven States of Perception: Primary Values*
9. *Spiritual and Cosmological Guide to the Personessence System*

ABOUT the AUTHOR

José Stevens, PhD, is an international lecturer, teacher, consultant, and trainer. A psychologist, licensed clinical social worker, and author of eighteen books and ebooks as well as numerous articles, he is also on the board of the Society of Shamanic Practitioners. He is the cofounder of the Power Path School of Shamanism and the Center for Shamanic Education and Exchange. He completed a ten-year apprenticeship with a Huichol *maracame* and has studied extensively with the Shipibos of the Amazon and the Q'ero of the Andes for the last twenty years.

He has a doctorate in Integral Counseling from the California Institute of Integral Studies, an MSW from the University of California, Berkeley, and a BA in sociology from the University of Santa Clara, California.

He lives in Santa Fe with his wife and task companion, Lena.